Change It Up!

Other Books by Amanda Dickson

Wake Up to a Happier Life

Change It Up!

Looking Differently at the Change You Want—
and the Change You Don't

AMANDA DICKSON

SHADOW
MOUNTAIN

Visit us at ShadowMountain.com

Library of Congress Cataloging-in-Publication Data

Dickson, Amanda.
    Change it up : looking differently at the change you want, and the change you don't / [Amanda Dickson].
        p.   cm.
    Includes bibliographical references.
    ISBN 978-1-60641-202-2 (hardbound : alk. paper)
    1. Change (Psychology)   2. Life change events.   3. Problem solving.
4. Decision making.   5. Self-help techniques.   I. Title.
    BF637.C4D49 2009
    155.2'4—dc22
                                                                              2009031841

Printed in the United States of America
R. R. Donnelley, Crawfordsville, IN

10   9   8   7   6   5   4   3   2   1

For Ashley

CONTENTS

Contents

INTRODUCTION

Ask most people how they feel about change, and they cringe. "Not today, thanks, and we're all booked up tomorrow, too."

Let's pause for a moment. Do you genuinely dislike change? You love the first chill in the air in the fall and the early buds coming up in the spring—those are changes. You love a new outfit or the smell of a new car—such fun changes. We enjoy changes we choose—not the ones chosen for us. We want to see change coming, but sometimes it is a gift hidden behind wrapping paper; we don't know what's in there. It could be something we'll really like. It could bless our lives in ways we might not have selected for ourselves, but that we'll embrace now that it's here. That's how gifts are—they catch us off-guard.

There is energy in change. Change, like all surprises, has a real charge to it. If it's energy you crave—and who doesn't—then change something. Today. Now. Change the way you look, the roads you drive on, the channel you watch. Change something and see everything light up, and lighten up, if only a bit. Chocolate and laughter may give you energy too, but if a real spark is what you seek, do something completely different and feel your engagement soar. Change is power.

Think of the stories you tell about your own life. There is the young you, the one from before you graduated from high school. Then you changed. You grew up. There's the you who had a career, possibly the first of many. Then you changed. Perhaps you got married. Perhaps you had children. That changed you forever. You hardly recognize yourself. And then there's the you who retired, whose children moved on to college and beyond. What a glorious time in your life. You define the eras of your life with change. It made you who you are today.

> "It is not the strongest of the species that survives, nor the most intelligent that survives. It is the one that is the most adaptable to change."
>
> CHARLES DARWIN

Change takes us out of our comfort zone and into the next room. We don't know who will be in that room, what the temperature will be, or if we'll like the way it smells. So what do we do? We assume we won't like it and try to avoid it. We rarely see change with "half-full" eyes instead of "half-empty" ones. Unexpected change could be the best thing that ever happened to us, but we rarely consider that. We may love learning how to be a parent (even at forty) as soon as the shock wears off. But, alas, there must be a *first* with every new activity—whether it's swimming or working or learning to live alone. And that first time means change.

Sometimes, change rocks our world to its foundation. But that's not always a bad thing. In nature, trees must shed their leaves, wildfires must clear out dense undergrowth, female bodies must go through racking changes to bring life. Life itself depends on the most unsubtle of changes. Yes, change can bring pain, but even pain can be appreciated. Pain can teach us gratitude, show us our humanity, bring us to our knees in a way we can only appreciate after the fact. Only after the initial injury of the change has passed do we see the value for what it is—the miracle of life. And if it helps ease the agony at all, remember that we are connected, one to another, in this common experience. It's like they say about life—no one is getting out alive. And no one is getting out unchanged.

Contrary to what you might have been thinking about some circumstance in your life, things should *not* remain the same. They should change, both radically and in small ways, every day. It's the process of life. It's what it means to be alive.

We face change—planned and unexpected—and it takes our breath away. That's what it's supposed to do. How do we let it do that without so much suffering and instead let it into our lives with maybe, just maybe, a little pleasure? How do we move from one stage to the next, from one state to the next, from one role to the next, without lamenting to the point of paralysis the loss of the stage we're leaving? That's what this book is all about.

If I had a wish for you, it would be for more change in your life because change *is* life.

Change is growth. It's sloughing off the old and welcoming the new. It's reinvigorating old relationships with new habits, old ways of thinking with new philosophies that blow our minds. Change is fun. Change is a dinner guest we didn't know was coming, a road closed that pushes us onto the loveliest side street we would never have discovered otherwise. Change is joy. Change is being and breath and vitality.

> "I believe that man's noblest endowment is his capacity to change."
>
> LEONARD BERNSTEIN

The only thing missing is our failure to see it that way and make peace with it.

CHAPTER ONE

"You Look So Great. Did You Change Your Hair?"

Let's start with the easy stuff.

I am a believer in starting slow and building. I hate to fail too much up front for fear of getting discouraged and never returning to the task. It's like skiing: start on the bunny hills. With change, let's start with the superficial, simple things you can do without any discomfort. Stuff you might even enjoy doing. I know this first chapter may seem shallow and unnecessary to some readers. Bear with me. Once you develop the skills to change, you can apply them to even the most difficult challenges thrown at you.

So, let's begin, literally, on the surface—with the way you look. Have you noticed how people tend to compliment you when you've changed something?

"You look so great. Have you lost weight?"

"Did you do something to your skin? Come on. Tell me what you did—you look so young."

"Have you been working out? When do you find the time?"

Have you ever noticed that people often compliment you on one thing, say losing weight, when it's actually something else you've changed, maybe

Change wakes you up.

your hair color? What's at work here? What is it about the change that inspires the compliment? It might *not* be that the person actually looks better. The old hair and the old clothes may have been just fine. It's the change that does it. Why?

Change wakes you up. Change enlivens you, enthuses you, brings energy into your being. You may not be aware of it, but other people certainly are. They feel it. That's why they compliment you.

Why not bring the energy of change into your appearance more often? Who knows, the energy may leak into other areas of your life, perhaps into more important areas. The changes don't need to be big, hairy ones. They don't even need to be changes you should make, for health or other reasons, like losing weight or cutting back on caffeine. Sometimes it's fun to just make changes for change's sake.

Women tend to first think of their hair. Sure. That's a

good one. Try another color or another cut or even just a ponytail. I started straightening my very unruly hair a year or so ago, a latecomer to the copycats of Jennifer Aniston. I love running my fingers through my long, straight locks now, always amazed that they are on my head—mine! My hair feels cleaner and more professional, when, in effect, it's neither—it's just straighter, changed.

What about for men? I don't know a man who thinks about changing his hairstyle, but he could, even if subtly. Try a different setting on the shaver—go 5 on the top and 3 on the sides—live dangerously.

The next easy change to try is wardrobe. I'm not suggesting anything drastic. You may not have much to choose from in your closet, and that may suit you just fine. I have one suggestion here—color. I don't know if you're like me, but I tend to wear black or cream T-shirts and turtlenecks under everything. My husband is even worse.

He owns ten T-shirts, and all but one are black. He looks so good in *Think outside the black.* color, but he doesn't wear it. He doesn't think he looks good in it. (He's wrong, of course.) But the point is, if he wants to embrace change, he's got to try out some color.

A year ago, a girlfriend of mine bought me an orange sweater—a color I can honestly say I have never purchased and *would* never purchase. (Who wears orange? What, is it

Halloween?) But what sweater do you think I get the most compliments on every time I wear it? Yep—the orange one. I need to think outside the black.

So add some color. Go buy T-shirts in different colors. Buy some with different fabrics. If you usually do V-neck, try crew neck. If you usually do white, try gray. Put aside the white Keds just for a day and put on a pair of red hightops. I'm not an image consultant, but I know what happens when you try something that *feels* different to you—you wake up. And if it also makes you look better or makes you *think* you look better, then you're in the bonus. But I'm not all that concerned with that part of it; I want you to have an easy experience with change. Trying a new look with your appearance can take the fear out of change.

Hmm. I thought I was going to look terrible with short hair, you think as your hairstylist twirls you around to see the back side. *But I look so cute.* You wonder why you didn't try it sooner. I wonder the same thing.

What things should you have tried sooner?

Maybe you have finally started taking the stairs instead of the elevator at work. It's not a full-blown workout, but it gets your body moving. You wonder why you didn't try it sooner. Maybe you wonder why you didn't start treating yourself to a carwash every week in the winter when your car is covered in salt and snow and slush. It's a few bucks, not more than you'd spend on lunch, and it makes you look forward, on some small level, to getting in the car and driving to work. Why didn't you try that sooner? What are the things bugging you right now that you wish were fixed?

You might think fixing the garage door or touching up the paint or calling the plumber is going to be such a pain, so you put it off. While you're putting it off, it's eating at you like a mental mosquito, buzzing around your consciousness, irritating your every waking moment. You wake up, and what's the first thing you think of? "I wish someone (not me) would get this garage door fixed."

> Things people often wish they had tried sooner:
>
> 1. Any form of exercise
> 2. Seeing a movie alone
> 3. Introducing themselves to someone
> 4. Learning any new technology (I love facebook!)
> 5. And the biggest one of all, forgiveness of anyone for anything

Just do it. Make a small change. It will comfort your everyday life.

Other easy changes can bring the same energy into your life. One of my favorites is decluttering. There is nothing as easy and empowering as getting rid of stuff. Oh, how I love to give stuff away! I go through my closets regularly and pull out things I think I won't wear anymore. Sometimes I'm wrong and wish I had it back, but only once every ten or twenty years. I give away shoes and belts and pants and coats.

I do the same thing to my young boys' closets, and I would to my teenagers' closets if they'd let me. I give away books and knickknacks, presents that I know I'll never use (that's not re-gifting, is it?), dishes and vases and everything I truly don't need. I do it all the time. It's a beautiful thing.

The opposite idea is to buy something, to bring something new into your living space. I like this change less, but I still like it. It can give you some great energy if you do it right and you can afford it. (Note: a new thing can *never* bring good energy if you can't afford to pay for it.) I bought my husband a new piece of art last year, something he loved (and that I happen to love too), and I felt the light in the room change. The spirit of the room, the way people feel in the room, is now altered. With one piece of art. The same thing can happen with pillows or a picture of your family, or even just cheap flowers from the grocery store. (My sister taught me that one. Thank you, Connie.) Five bucks of flowers can fill a room with life that everyone benefits from, whether they notice the flowers or not.

Do You Mind If I Change the Channel?

I'm not talking about channel surfing—that disengaged flipping through endless channels and not really seeing anything that appears on the screen (although I know my husband would argue there is real value to that kind of browsing). I'm talking about changing your habit. If you always watch ABC News, try NBC. If you always watch *Good Morning America,* try the *Today Show.* Watch something different than you usually do. Listen to something different than you usually do. Try a different radio station. (It hurts to suggest that, since I'm a radio announcer. Forgive the self-interest, but if you live in Utah, you can try other stations, but you must come back to KSL.) Listen to different music. Listen to each other.

If you always drive to work by taking one side street to the same entrance to the same freeway, try something else. Take an entirely different route and forget about which is closer. See different stores, different neighborhood restaurants. If you always stop at a certain gas station to fill up, try a different one. If you usually never go in, walk in, look around, and buy something small. If you're like me, I always sit in the same chair at the dining table for every meal at home. My husband sits across from me and the kids sit all around, however many of them are there. Let's change that.

> **Five simple things you can change today (Why not?)**
>
> 1. Get up a half-hour earlier (or later—it's the change we're going for here).
> 2. If you usually brush your teeth before you get in the shower, do it after.
> 3. Switch the place you park—with your spouse at home, or at work.
> 4. Change your flavor of gum.
> 5. Change your perfume or deodorant—get a new smell going.

I'm going to sit where Ethan usually sits and move everybody one seat to the left! They'll never get over it. It will be a blast. (I would consider asking my husband to sleep on the other side of the bed, but you can take this change business only so far!)

The energy of change is exactly why the change-up pitch is so successful in baseball. The pitcher throws a pitch that looks exactly like the fast ball he just threw, same angle, same position of hand on the ball, only it's ten miles an hour slower. Just that little bit of change throws everything off, messes up the batter's timing, and often leads to "Steeee-riiiiike!"

Oh, the power of change—in sports, in closets, in life. It's the influence on your whole being that comes from shifting the smallest thing.

I know such things may seem too small to be significant. Don't judge right now. Just ride a bike somewhere, anywhere, and see how different everything looks from that seat you may not have sat on for years.

Five more small things you can change:

1. Read in a different chair in your house.
2. Buy a different kind of bread.
3. Play music when you normally have silence and have silence when you normally play music.
4. Put on different comfy clothes when you get home from work.
5. Once a week, always on a different day, wake one of your kids up early just to have breakfast with him or her.

Remember the powerful movie, *Dead Poets Society*? There is a scene near the beginning when Robin Williams's character invites his class of young male English students to come to the front of the classroom and step onto his desk, one at a time, look out over the class, then step down. He invites them to do it because the view is different from there.

Exactly.

Playing Out the Worst-Case Scenario

What will happen if I cut my hair or change my wardrobe or my job . . . or my life? I may hate it. I may love it, mind you, but I may hate it. When we're afraid of the unknown that change can bring, we go to worst-case scenarios in our minds, and those scenarios scare us off. Many a dream has disappeared in the fog of "what will happen if . . . ?" followed by horror stories. There are a few fallacies at work here in these worst-case scenarios.

1. If I don't change, nothing bad will happen.
2. If I do change, the worst thing will happen.
3. I won't like the worst thing.

Let's look at each one.

One, there is the assumption that if I don't choose change, no change will come, and then everything will be hunky-dory. If I don't seek change out, it won't find me. I'll be in control. I'll always look and feel the way I do now. Nothing bad will happen to me or to anyone I love. If I fear change, then I must feel pretty comfortable with the status quo. I want to keep it, preserve it, get away from this talk of change. While my life may not be perfect, at least I understand this set of challenges. I know how to do this.

But change does not ask our permission before it enters. And often, change isn't a gradual process. It gives us no time to prepare, no time to adjust. Our husband leaves, or our mother dies, or our child is diagnosed with autism. You aren't afforded the opportunity to worry about these events. They just happen. If you are alive, there is no place where you are safe from change. Whether you seek it out or not, it's coming.

> **The three fallacies of change**
>
> 1. If I don't change, nothing bad will happen.
> 2. If I do change, the worst thing will happen.
> 3. I won't like the worst thing.

The second and most obvious fallacy of the worst-case scenario is believing that the worst thing will, in fact, happen if you embrace change. Let's be clear about this—it might *not* happen.

It might, mind you, but it might not. If you sign up for swimming lessons at age forty-seven, you might feel so mortified that your whole body turns red for the first five minutes, until you meet the other three women and one man who decided that they, too, wanted to learn what their children had known since they were three.

If you trust your daughter with the car, she actually might drive safely and come home on time (and feel more self-worth because you trusted her). If you write the book you've always wanted to write, maybe no one will want to publish it. You just might spend years writing and editing and sending query letters to agents who will, if you're lucky, take the time to turn you down. Or, you may meet someone who sees the value of your words and wants to publish them. It *could* happen! When you get in the car in the morning, do you think about how someone might run a red light and smash into you, leaving you paralyzed for life? I hope not.

> We never think about the best case scenario. Ask yourself, "What is the best thing that could happen to me if this happens?" Think about three changes you're experiencing right now and ask yourself that question for all three.

We've got to get our energy away from worst-case scenarios which, after all, might not happen, and meanwhile are robbing us of the energy we need for life.

The third fallacy of change, and of the worst-case scenario specifically, is that you won't like the change. You believe that if the "worst" thing happens to you, there is no way you're going to like it. ("That's kind of obvious, Amanda. How could I like the worst thing?") It's not possible you'll like your hair after it's "ruined," your life without your former "best friend" in it, taking the bus because you lost your car, being without the job you've had for twenty years. How could you? How could you like being alone or suffering or not having any money? What could be good about any of those states?

This is the most counter-intuitive fallacy of the three. But go with me for a moment. Have you heard of people who have said cancer saved their lives? They were walking around dead to themselves, to their families and their own spirits, until they were jolted by a life-threatening diagnosis, and now they are grateful for their bout with cancer. I've known people who feared getting fired, who went into work every day with the thought that "today might be the day they blow me out," only to realize their worst fear: they got fired, and then they found their dream job. Haven't you known someone who is terrified that her boyfriend will break up with her, and then he does? Your jilted friend is distraught for a day, a week, a month, and then meets the man she always wanted to be with, a true soul mate, the man she would have missed had the jerk not dumped her in the first place?

The worst-case scenario is just a change, and sometimes it's a change for the better, a change you'll be grateful for one day. It's a different route to work, a different color of sweater. That's all. It is the unknown. We fear it because we haven't experienced it yet. The future frightens us for this very reason. We don't know what it will hold. It may be paradise, but we haven't seen it yet, so we're afraid there won't be enough parking spaces. In Charles Dickens's *A Christmas Carol,* Scrooge was most frightened by the Ghost of Christmas Future, the spirit whose face he could not see within the black cloak. He wasn't frightened by the pain of his past. He knew that pain. And he wasn't frightened by the suffering of his present. He was familiar with that. It was the unforeseeable in his future that this toughened old man could not face. The future did him in (and therein blessed him).

> What is the worst thing that has ever happened to you? How has it made you who you are today? What has it taught you? In what ways would you not be you without that challenge? In other words, how has it blessed you?

This is how we are with change. We hide from it behind cloaks and jobs and bad relationships, but we only need remember to get up on the desk and see the room differently.

If this guy dumps me, and I wind up being free to make new friends and fall in love with someone more deserving, I am blessed.

If this boss fires me, then I am free to find my passion and earn a living in a more fulfilling environment—so I am blessed.

If I lose something about my health that I have taken for granted, then I will cherish life in a way I never have before, and I will help others to do the same.

And I am blessed.

CHAPTER TWO
"Who's That Girl?"

I'm in the ambulance on my way to the emergency room with what I later will understand is appendicitis when the EMT who is riding with me says, "Wait. Aren't you that girl on the radio?"

"Yeeeesssssss," I manage to get out before erupting with some sort of controlled scream.

"I listen to you every morning!" he responds happily. I'm afraid he's going to continue this line of discussion.

"Thank you." My voice sounds like a gurgle. I'm not sure if I'm flattered or if I want to pursue having his license pulled.

Meeting a listener of my radio program is normally something I'm pleased with, something I'm grateful for, but at this particular moment, when I feel like I might be dying, I'd rather not talk shop. I'd rather just be Amanda, the patient.

Amanda, the one who now knows her scream is horror-movie quality.

"Ya know, I've always wanted to know something about you." Apparently, this is an average day for this guy; my screams don't make a dent in him. "Are you really that happy all the time?" He's laughing now.

"Not at the moment." *Obviously.* I plot his death.

I have these experiences from time to time when I feel very strongly about my work identity. I happen to be a radio announcer; that's one of my titles. I am known to many people in my home state of Utah because of my job. This identity blesses my life, and my family's lives, in countless ways. I have the opportunity to meet interesting people, attend extraordinary happenings, and sometimes use what celebrity status I have for good when I contribute my time and endorsement to causes and events.

But occasionally I would just like to be anonymous, like when my toddler has "an accident" on the carpet in the dentist's office. But before I start sounding like a whiny celebrity (which I'm not! Just ask my glam squad!), the reason I share this story with you is to talk about the labels or titles we give ourselves and how they change.

Who are you now? Are you proud and pleased with the roles you play, or do they shame you and make you want to cringe just at the thought of them? How would you identify yourself? If I were to answer that question, I'd say I am a mother, a wife, an employee, a writer, a woman, a sister, an aunt, a daughter.

I am a neighbor, a cousin, an infrequent runner, a laundry goddess, an incompetent shopper, and an insecure cook. ("Does it taste all right? Are you sure? You know, if it doesn't, we can always order pizza.") These are the titles I give myself, but they may not be the titles others give me.

I know some of my friends would describe me as a generous friend (God bless them) and a workaholic. My kids might think of me as a remote control device and juice dispenser. It has been my experience that no matter what I weigh, I usually describe myself as fat and my husband (smart man) describes me as thin. I know other people who would call me a

> Write a list of your titles.
> Who are you today?
> What are the roles you play?
> How many can you think of?

phony nincompoop, an insincere cheerleader, and a condescending sycophant. (I've read it in their blogs. Ouch!) Here's the interesting thing about all of these labels.

None of them is really me.

How do I know that? Because titles *change.* They come and go and come back again, but *I'm still here.*

"I" am here whether I'm a wife or not, whether I'm a radio announcer or not, whether I'm a daughter or not, whether I'm a nincompoop or not. Who are you after you get divorced and no longer have the title of *wife* or *husband?* Who are you after you get fired or your children grow up and move away or you lose your house and the neighbors you have come to love so much?

We'll talk in this chapter about how labels have changed in your life and how you might want to consciously change them in the future. We'll think about how you can let go of the labels you have ingrained into your mind-set.

What are some of the titles people have assigned to you? Others see us so differently than we see ourselves. What labels would your spouse, your children, your coworkers, or your grocer give you?

"I've always been a worry wart. That's just who I am." That may be true for who you've been, but it may not be true for who you are *becoming.* Changing even life-long labels will not be as scary as it might have once been because you'll remember the one constant—the one constant is *you.*

You are always there in whatever role you're playing. Only the *titles* are subject to change—you the worrier, you the mother, you the wife, you the teacher. But *you* are the constant. You are unchanging, even as the wind swirls around you. Take interest in the wind. Notice it. Ride it when you please, but do not confuse yourself with it.

You are not your titles. You are not your roles. You are not the actions you take or the ways people count on you. You are simply you—pure, beautiful, you.

Changing the Labels

Your titles have been changing for as far back as you can remember. In grade school, you may have had the label of good student or troublemaker or class clown or ballplayer. Your teachers might have described you as a natural athlete or not as gifted as your older brother or smarter than you were letting on. You may have always thought of yourself as an "A" student, or a "C" student barely getting by. Were any of these labels true? I can think of times in my life when very few of the titles I possessed seemed to accurately describe me.

Is there a label you currently have that doesn't feel right to you? A label you might want to change?

During the years when I was a lawyer, for instance, I felt like an impostor almost every day. I felt like I wasn't in my own life, in my own clothes, in my own skin.

Now that you've identified some of your titles, some of your identities, let's talk about changing them. As you grew up, you naturally changed. You became a boyfriend or girlfriend, a teenager, a driver. You became a high school graduate, maybe a college student, then possibly a wife or husband. You might have become a parent (a sacred role we can do well or poorly, but that never changes), a homeowner or a member of the PTA. Later you might have laid some of those labels aside, become a condominium owner, a retired teacher, a grandmother, a philanthropist. Hold all of those labels in your heart for a moment, the ones you possessed as a young person and the ones you possess today.

You can almost feel a kindness toward the labels of your earlier years. When you remember being a nervous freshman in college, can you feel empathy for that role? When you recollect the new bride or groom, the first-time parent, the small-business owner taking out her first loan, can you remember what donning that hat felt like? You might remember nervous sweats, insecurity, worry that you wouldn't be good enough. Don't you wish you could hug that person, that "you" of your youth, and tell her not to worry so much?

So many of our roles change naturally, seemingly without any intervention from us. As we age, we just become different people. But what about the roles we can consciously affect? We can reinvent ourselves any time we want to, add roles, take roles away, change our identities entirely. Let's say you've always had the role of someone who judges others. That's been your role. You've been judging people since you learned how from your mother thirty years ago. You don't mean to be mean. You just call 'em as you see 'em.

But now you see your daughter starting to judge people. You see her say things about their weight and their beliefs and their ethnicity and their poverty, and you hear yourself in her voice. You cringe. This is not what you wanted to teach her. When she was a baby, you dreamed about teaching her how to love life, to dance, to love other people, especially those less fortunate than she. Ah-hah. You have just been blessed with a moment when the label you've been wearing has run smack into the one you want to wear.

What do you do now? Shrug your shoulders and say, "Well, that's just the way I am. I can't do anything about the way I was brought up"? Or do you take this opportunity to consciously change your identity? Changing is not as hard as you may believe. I know you've been thinking the other way your whole life, talking the other way your whole life. But we're focusing on the rest of your life now. And that is up to you, not dictated by anything in your past, no matter how deep the rut.

> "The only human institution which rejects progress is the cemetery."
> HAROLD WILSON

What an exciting place! You get to decide what your next role will be. It's almost like taking on a new job. If you become a teacher or a consultant or a home business entrepreneur, you change. Your title changes, and with it come changes to your everyday experience. Similarly, if you've been

Five roles you could change today with a simple decision to make it so:

1. Person who always orders dessert changes to a person who does so only once in a while.
2. Person who is always late changes to a person who is always on time.
3. Person who doesn't like exercise changes to a person who finds a kind of exercise he likes.
4. Person who never votes changes to a person who votes in the next election.
5. Person who doesn't cook changes to a person who buys a cookbook, follows the steps, and discovers how easy it is!

a grouch your whole life, snipping at everything and everyone for the most minor infractions, you don't have to keep choosing that role. You could fire yourself from the job of Grinch and try something new.

Maybe you'll just try not judging the next bit of news you receive. When you hear, "Mom, I'm dropping out this semester," instead of saying, "I just knew it. I just knew you would never follow through with anything. What do you expect to make of yourself without a college education?" you could ask, "Why, honey?" and let that be the beginning of a valuable discussion, for both of you.

The Role of Victim—The Role You Were Not Born to Play

If there is one identity I will go so far as to encourage you to change, it is the label of *victim*. We hear a lot about the victim role. You've heard it on *Oprah* and every other talk show that discusses relationships or self-improvement. I find in my own experience that there is at least a little victim in all of us.

"Poor me—I have to work."

"Poor me—I have to take care of the kids."

"Poor me—I have so much homework to do."

The flip sides to those laments are—you have a job, you lucky son of a gun. You have children, you blessed woman. You get to go to college, you privileged young man. Same experience. Different interpretation. One without the "victim."

I see two ways out of getting stuck in the victim role. They are gratitude and forgiveness. Sometimes—usually—I need both. If I have been wronged by someone, or perceive that I have been wronged, I need forgiveness. And the sooner the better. There is no such thing as forgiving too soon. I know sometimes you'll think, "Well, he really hurt me. I need to chew on this for a while." No. You don't. You could forgive right then, immediately, if you wanted to. There is no length of time you should make yourself suffer in that identity, no protocol of victimhood.

And you probably know by now that resenting whoever hurt you does nothing to get back at the offender. They're not usually even aware of your resentment. Forgiveness is not something you do for the offender. It has nothing to do with whether or not the other person even deserves it. You do it for *you,* for your freedom, for your life.

Just another word here about forgiveness. I have come to think of forgiveness as a morning ritual. I include it with brushing my teeth. I think of it like this: I wake up. I take a shower. I brush my teeth. I forgive. That's it.

Who do I have to forgive today? Often I think of some slight I perceived from one of my kids or a coworker, some unfair circumstance I encountered. Most days it's something I need to forgive myself for. I worked too late and didn't spend enough time with my family. Ahhh. I'll forgive myself. I'll do better today.

I like to do my forgiveness in the morning for the same reason that people do their exercise in the morning—it gets your metabolism going. I want to get my forgiveness metabolism going so if some unexpected slight comes upon me later in the day (and aren't they always unexpected?), I'll be warmed up and ready to forgive on the spot. See how this works?

Now, if you're just beginning this process, you have to eat the elephant one bite at a time. If you've got teenagers, you won't be able to do all your forgiving in one morning or you'll be late for work. Just work on a few items today, then a few the next day, and then a few more the next. My goal is to wake up one day and after I put the toothpaste on the toothbrush (the kind for sensitive teeth), I won't be able to think of anything or anyone to forgive. I'll run through all the people who usually push my buttons, picturing their faces with their most annoying expressions. I'll tilt my head to one side and then to the other, and I genuinely won't feel like I need to forgive anyone.

Hallelujah! You've come a long way, baby.

The Man in the Mirror

Remember the famous pop song, "The Man in the Mirror"? The lyrics point out that if we want to change the world, we have to look at ourselves first and change! Oh, I used to sing along so loudly to that song on the radio. Nothing like a little music to inspire the changing soul!

I have looked at myself in the mirror and wondered, "Who is that girl? Where did *I* go?" I don't recognize myself sometimes, and it scares me. Am I still in there? Is the little girl who read *The Secret Garden* and dreamed of being an Olympic swimmer still in there? I wonder how I got like this, so consumed with casserole recipes, so . . . middle-aged. I still marvel when I pause to remember that I am a mother now. When little ones say "Mommy," they could be talking to me! I am responsible for other people's lives, their health, their futures. Where is the carefree me who used to stay up late watching movies, eating burritos at all hours and sleeping until noon?

She's still there. She is me. She is part of the unchanging

"I" inside the labels. I know that now. Sometimes I just need to remind myself. She is still me. She has been here all along and ever will be. She is the one nudging me to make a change—now—for the better. She may want to experience another part of this sweet life, one my fear and insecurity have been denying her.

"I'm looking at the man in the mirror. I'm asking him to make a change." This may be your soul's song to you. If so, let it sink in. See the change for what it is—another way to work, a different color sweater, a role you hadn't contemplated before that may become your favorite. You can do this. Change isn't the scary monster you thought it was as a child. You are getting good at opening up to this now. Bring it on, baby! What else ya got?

CHAPTER THREE

"The One Thing You Can Count on Is Change" *Yada Yada Yada*

You've seen them all before. The bumper sticker lines:

"The one thing you can count on is change."

"The more things change, the more they stay the same."

"Change is inevitable, except from vending machines." (Okay, maybe not that one.)

We know in our brains that these mantras are true— that's why they're mantras. But somehow, even as we say the words, we tighten. We don't really want to change. Change could mean something we don't like. Change could mean pain, or ultimately even death. Change brings up all the fears of the unknowable future, and we'd rather just keep things the same. We don't have time for change. We're just too busy!

Let's daydream for a moment. Think back to the most amazing experience of your life. What was it? Was it climbing a mountain with your brother, extending yourself well beyond what you thought you were capable of? Was it skiing or sky-diving or the day you got married? Was it the birth of your first child and the miracle of being there at that moment when God is most undeniably present?

Whatever it was, I bet it wasn't something you'd done a thousand times before. The most amazing experience of your life was likely something you were doing for the first time. You opened yourself to a new experience. You spent your first day as a nonsmoker and held the new baby who in-spired you to quit. You loved with a fully open and non-judgmental heart and, in doing so, saw your husband for the first time. You fell on your knees in hu-mility after your daughter came back to you. These powerful moments, life-elevating moments, would not have happened without change.

You may decide to change the way you feel about change today.

And yet we fear change.

Or we used to. Just because you've pushed change away from you in the past doesn't mean you will do it tomorrow. You may decide to change the way you feel about change to-day. Why not? What's stopping you?

There are people out there—and I know many of them—who say and mean, "I love change." You could be one of these people. You just need a little confidence with the process, a few good experiences with change to show how pain-free it can be, a few successes to help you forget the difficult experiences of your earlier years. Then you'll be set to fly solo and even teach others.

Rip It Off!

Change is like a Band-Aid. It's good to change something small fast. Just rip it off. Right now, move the books on your desk somewhere else. Give them to the library. Throw them away. (I know, throwing away books is blasphemous, but we've got to change something in your everyday environment.) Throw away some of those awards you don't care about that are stacked up against your window or the knick-knacks that clutter your shelves. Dust something, for crying out loud! Put down this book and go buy new plants, as many as you can afford, and fill your house and office with them. Or take all the plants you have and give them to your neighbors. Burn this book or rip out all the pages and throw them up in the air.

I don't care what you change. The audacity of doing something so totally different will help you more than anything I have to say in the next chapters. Cut your long fingernails off. Shave your beard. Paint your new short fingernails bright pink. Throw your doors and windows open and let the fresh air fill your home until the neighbors wonder what you're up to.

Jump into change, small, little, unintimidating change. Don't worry *what* you change. The *what* doesn't matter at all, as long as it doesn't hurt anybody. I am not arguing for the merit of one change versus another. I don't care what it is. What I care about is helping you see the value—and the pleasure—in the new, the different, the change itself. Buy a new purse or a new backpack for school. Take everything out of the old and put it into the new, then give the old to charity.

> What have you always wanted to learn? Sign up for a class today! (You can always drop out later if it turns out not to be for you.)
>
> Piano lessons
> Pottery
> Motorcycle riding
> Tae kwon do

Sign up for a knitting class. Don't just *think* that it sounds like a good idea. Go online, find one in your area, and *sign up for it!* Commit yourself in writing to attending the class.

Better yet, pay some money for it. That'll get you to actually *go*. Learning new skills and talents is not just for children. Part of what keeps us alive is the inherent thrill and change of learning something new. If you haven't learned a new skill in a while (or thirty years) then you are way overdue.

Here's my confession of a late learner. I took my first

skiing lesson at age thirty-four. (I had been skiing once before with my brother when I was eighteen, but I figure that sliding down the mountain on my backside for three hours—cursing him all the way—doesn't count.) My first skiing lesson was literally life-elevating. Once I got past getting my boots and bindings and gear all fitted, and stood up, and then learned how to walk without falling, and then glided ever so slightly without falling, and then got on the chair lift without falling, and then glided snow-plow style without falling, and then learned how to fall . . . it was thrilling. It was being a toddler again, learning how to walk. It was allowing myself to be vulnerable enough to need someone to help me stand up.

Learning new skills and talents is not just for children.

It was risky, so risky. I might have stunk. I might have embarrassed myself. But I loved it! It was a respect for my body I hadn't felt in many years. It was respect for the power and beauty of Mother Nature. And it was entirely new. I changed! I went from being the girl who lived in Utah who didn't know how to ski to the Utah girl who just learned how to ski. (By the way, both kinds of girls are fine; it's the change I underwent that I'm celebrating here.)

One of the best changes you can make may feel small, but isn't. Extend yourself in the service of someone else. My sister, Connie, taught me this. If you want to get some momentum with change, start by doing something for someone else. Maybe a neighbor of yours has been sick and seems overwhelmed with her kids. Offer to take them for the afternoon. Tell her you've got a day in the park planned and your big kids can help watch her little ones. Even if she says no, she'll know that maybe she can lean on you in the future. Just that phone call may make a change in both of your lives. Or would it really kill you, when you're making a chocolate pie this weekend, to mix up the filling for a second pie and take it to the man down the street who lives alone now and is probably sick of the taste of store-bought everything? Small acts on your part may have huge consequences in terms of the love felt on both sides.

If you want something less intimate, and many people do, think of a cause that captures your heart and do something to benefit that cause today. Send money to a worthy organization. Sign up for—and do—a 5K walk or run. Read a website about an issue you've been interested in, and sign up for their newsletter. Watch *Oprah* and act on some of the suggestions she makes. It's the *doing* we're going for here, not just the learning, because in the doing, in the taking of the action step, something magical is born.

I cannot tell you how many people I have known whose entire lives are locked in the thought process which immediately precedes the action step. They have spent years thinking about losing weight, years wanting to apologize to their father, years wanting to move to California or New York or abroad. They have spent decades wondering what it would be like to be politically active, but instead of doing something about it, they just complain to their kids all the time and never . . . actually . . . do . . . anything! They never even vote.

I may be wrong, but I think they don't do anything because all they see are the poles. At the North Pole are those who are doing nothing, and clear over there at the South Pole are those who are changing the world. They don't value the thousands of steps between the poles. Meanwhile, I rarely think about anything but the small steps in between. When I decided to write this book, I didn't consider whether I had enough ideas to fill a whole book. I just knew I was fascinated with the topic of change, so I began writing. Chapter one led to chapter two, and so on. Don't let the fear of not making it to the end stop you from taking the next step.

Don't let the fear of not making it to the end stop you from taking the next step.

What Else Ya Got?

If you changed something small just now, or recently, you felt how easy it was. You also felt a little rush from it, didn't you? The smallest change in our environment, or in our way of thinking, can give a real spiritual lift. We need that. We need the energy of small changes to help us get the momentum we'll need for the bigger, more challenging changes to come.

I want you to hang out in small-change land for as long as you need to until you feel confident. Change small things in every room in your house. Change your wardrobe. Change your grocery store, your yogurt brand, and your water bottle. Change what you read in the morning and what you watch at night. Keep changing and changing and changing until your heart asks, "What else ya got?"

Now you're ready.

You're ready for the biggest change I know: I want to suggest you change what happiness means to you. Up until this day, happiness may have meant one thing very specifically defined by you. It may have meant marrying a man who had no children and had never been married before, and then living together happily ever after. It may have meant making millions of dollars and owning six cars and living in a mansion. It may have meant keeping one job for the rest of your life. It may have meant looking like Brad Pitt or Angelina Jolie. It may have meant writing a best-selling novel and becoming famous all over the world.

Happiness is what is happening right now.

Those may have been dreams, but they were more than that. They were your definitions of happiness. Anything that didn't match up with those definitions was, therefore, un-happiness. Right?

Wrong. After making all those small changes, today you might be ready to change your definition of happiness. Try this one on: happiness is what is happening right now. It's this moment. As you're reading this book, there is happiness. As you're listening to your teenagers arguing downstairs, there is happiness. As you're worrying about your husband losing his job, there is happiness.

You know how after you suffer one of the biggest challenges of your life, you often look back years later with fondness or even laughter at what you went through? You marvel at how one of the worst times in your life could lead to one of the best times in your

> "I am always doing that which I cannot do, in order that I may learn how to do it."
>
> PABLO PICASSO

life. The trick to finding the happiness in those moments is to laugh sooner, not to wait for years to pass until the lightness lifts you up. Learn that trick today.

Don't get me wrong. I'm not suggesting you live in La-La Land. I understand that life will still have difficulty and pain and fear, but underneath and at the end of all of that, there is still happiness. Not cotton-candy, polka-dot happiness, but the real kind. The kind that doesn't depend upon perfection.

This kind of happiness doesn't mean giving up on, or giving

in, or letting go of your dreams. It does mean waking up to the dream you're already living. There is nothing "settling" about it. Happiness for you looks exactly like your life right now. It has your family, with all of its challenges. It has your body, your hair, your clothes. It has your job, or your lack of a job. It has your skills and education and interests. It has your health or illness, your children's health or illness. It even has some fear in it, but hopefully less than before you started reading this book. This is what happiness looks like for you . . . until it looks different.

Never let dreams tell you when you're allowed to be happy.

And it will. Oh, yes, it will. Tomorrow your happiness will look different than it does today, especially if you are able to embrace all the change that life brings. Your happiness in a year or in five years or more will look quite different than it does today. It might include some of those dreams that used to define your happiness—about the marriage and the body and the money—or it may not.

There is nothing wrong with dreaming. I do it all the time, every day. But never let dreams tell you when you're allowed to be happy. Dreams work for me, not the other way around. Happiness is something I've chosen to have in my life, every day, no matter what. Happiness is like being on time—it's a choice I made a long time ago, and one I made just ten minutes ago. And happiness needs change to breathe.

Happiness that depends on anything staying the same is not really happiness. It's just some counterfeit contentment that

Happiness that depends on anything staying the same is not really happiness.

will blow up the second somebody spills the milk.

You're Ready

If what is happening right now feels happy to you, then you're ready. You're ready for big change, in your mind and in your circumstance. I find those two usually go together. When the student is ready, the teacher will appear. I have no idea what big change will look like in your life, but I know it will be beautiful.

In my life, it looked like motherhood. I fell in love with a man in my late thirties who had three children from his first marriage. I fell completely in love with him, but I was terrified of the thought of being a stepmother. I had seen all the movies with the "evil stepmother," always maligned, dreaded, unappreciated. I didn't want to be her. Before he proposed, Aaron asked me, "Do you want to be a stepmother?"

I knew my answer to that question would determine if he would ever propose. "I'm not sure," I answered honestly, if not too quickly.

"Well, you'd better be sure, because my children are my

life." What a true and inspiring statement. It stopped me cold. One night a few weeks later, we dropped the kids off at their mother's house at dusk and drove away. We held hands on top of the stick shift.

"I want to be a stepmother," I said quietly, but not so quietly he couldn't hear me. He didn't say anything. He just cried.

And I did, too . . . I *wanted* to be a stepmother. It wasn't just something I was saying to please him. Since we married six years ago and I took on this sacred role, I have made many, many mistakes. I have tried at times to love his children too imposingly, I have cooked too elaborately, bought them too many toys. I have expected too much in return, been disappointed when they didn't say anything to me on Mother's Day, and wished they would say "I love you" back. All of those things were mistakes, weaknesses on my part, but I'm learning. I'm learning how to love them, truly and exactly as they are, and no learning process has ever been so filled with change.

And grace.

It is my belief that the exact love necessary for me to embrace becoming a stepmother is the reason I got pregnant for the first time at thirty-nine. I had come to believe that I wasn't able to have children of my own. That was not something I ever confirmed medically. I didn't want to hear the words, but it was my working theory. I was so confident in it, though, that I shared it with Aaron before we got married. As a result of that, the only person more surprised than I was when the pregnancy test came back positive was Aaron.

"But . . . I thought you said . . . you couldn't get pregnant," he said as he struggled to breathe.

"I know," I giggled. "I didn't think I could."

You want to talk about change? Try having your first baby at forty and your second at forty-three. Like the old joke goes, I know now why you're supposed to have your babies before you're forty . . . because you'll forget where you left them!

I think about my life five years ago, and I hardly recognize it. The changes have been thorough, profound, and miraculous. I believe this kind of change is what can happen when you see happiness in your life right now, exactly as it is, with all of its mess and mayhem. I am convinced I would not have recognized Aaron as my mate, would not have embraced my role as stepmother, and would not have been able to have these two beautiful sons if I had gotten stuck on my "dream" of happiness—because *my* dream, sure as the hole in a doughnut, didn't look like this. But that's only because I was too small to trust life. I'm bigger now. As the Ghost of Christmas Present sang in *Scrooge,* the musical version of *A Christmas Carol,* "I like life. Life likes me. Life and I fairly fully agree. Life is fine. Life is good. 'Specially mine which is just as it should be."

CHAPTER FOUR

"I Could Handle Anything but This. Not This"

There has likely been a day in your life, perhaps more than one, when a change crushed your bones. The longer we live, the more of these we face. "I could handle anything but this," we think . . . right up until the moment when we are forced to handle it.

Somehow. Somehow we keep breathing until the day ends, and another day comes, and we keep breathing some more. Somehow we incorporate the change into our skin. Somehow.

We are never the same after the day we are told we have cancer. Never the same. Every day we live after that, whether we are in pain or completely asymptomatic, is different. Every day is borrowed time. We put pain in perspective after a diagnosis like that. We look at our children differently, our work, our backyards. It's all changed. Likewise, we are never the same after the day we learn our child has an illness or a profound disability, the day we learn our precious little one will suffer or not be able to experience a full life (at least in the limited way we have defined "full" before now). What we value, what we wish for in our wildest dreams ("Let him just take one bite, just one bite of food and I'll be happy"), what we think when we see someone else's child running, is completely changed.

Who are we when our bodies are not perfect? Who are we when we can't live without a tube or a bag or a machine? Who is our son when he can't grow or walk or speak without drastic intervention? What kind of life is that?

"What kind of life is that?" is a question you ask before illness or disability happens to you. Not after. We fear what we don't understand. I am sure that I looked at children with disabilities earlier in my life and felt sorry for them or for their parents. "How sad for them," I can vaguely remember thinking. I am ashamed to admit that now. Forgive me. I knew not what I did. I am now the proud mother of two children with disabilities. My oldest daughter is Down Syndrome and my youngest son has Noonan's Syndrome (a condition I am still coming to understand). I am a member now of a club no parent would ever want to join, and yet it's a club I am not the least bit ashamed of, the club of parents of children with disabilities. It is an exclusive club, one where the dues are understanding and the meetings are whenever you need us. Laurel and Aiden, my two children, bless me and enrich me and humble me as my other children do, and perhaps more, because they take me beyond the fear I had once known.

I remember being pregnant with my youngest son and having the terror every mother, especially every older mother, has. "Please, God, don't let anything be wrong with the baby." This was my constant prayer. After Aiden was born, I had a nagging feeling that something was wrong, though nothing appeared to be to my untrained eye. When the doctor found a heart murmur at his two-month checkup, he sent me to a cardiologist. The cardiologist sent me to a geneticist. The geneticist came back in the room with several doctors, interns, social workers, and asked if my husband could be present.

"He can't be here today. I'm sorry," I answered, panic setting in. "What's wrong?"

They all kept talking around the problem, afraid I would fall apart, I suppose. That's probably why they brought the social worker.

"You better tell me right now because I'm losing courage," I finally blurted out.

My life changed forever the moment I heard Aiden's diagnosis. The mother I was, the person I was, the things I would spend my time doing and caring about, all changed in that instant. My thoughts raced to fears years in the future. Would he ever be able to go to college, get married, have children of his own? Would he live to see the first grade or the fifth? Would I be able to care for him well enough? What was God thinking, giving me this child? I know they say God doesn't give you a challenge you can't handle, but how strong does he think I am? My worst nightmare was coming true. I sobbed to myself as I started the car's engine, then I turned it off. I got out and went to the backseat and sat next to Aiden. He was already getting sleepy and closing his eyes. I had nursed him in the examination room before I left the hospital.

Perfect. That is the word that came to my mind. He was perfect. He, with his syndrome and his heart problems and his uncertain life, was perfect. Is my life any more certain than his? No. Is Ethan or Cameron or any of my other children's lives more certain? No. Our lives are all fragile and uncertain. Isn't that part of what makes them magical? I thought about how I had loved him two hours before, before I knew he was a child with a "diagnosis." Did I love him any less now? Of course not. Maybe I loved him more. I wept, quietly so as not to wake him, and my heart broke wide open. My life changed in that minute in the cold parking lot of Primary Children's Medical Center. I became a woman who loves what is.

Who are you now that you cannot walk without assistance? Who are you if you need medication to live without pain? Who are you now that you have to feed your child through a tube for the rest of her life? Do these physical limitations change who you are? They change you, for sure, but do they change who you *are*? Do they change the *you* underneath the labels? They change your routine and your experience and your circumstances, yes. What you spend your time doing will change, at least in part. You will have to think about things that other people don't, take things into account, plan. You may have to ask for help, lean on others, let them in. And the one thing you'll have to do at some point is forgive.

Who Will You Need to Forgive?

Everyone. For everything. I started with forgiving the doctors for telling me the news. That was an easy one. Then I moved to forgiving God. A much harder one. I know I shouldn't even think a thought like that, but I did. I blamed God. How could he do this to my child? I judged what he had done, and I blamed him. And when I finally stopped doing that, I moved to me. I blamed me. It must be my fault. If there is something wrong with Aiden, it must be because I was too old to have him, too sick. How could I have been so selfish as to get pregnant with a second child in my forties? A second child! Was one perfect miracle baby not enough?

I had to push it, didn't I? If I just hadn't been so selfish! I worked too much. I drank too many Diet Cokes. I didn't sleep enough. I did something that led to his having this condition which may cause a life of suffering.

The weeping seemed never-ending. I would wake up, and the crying would begin minutes after I gained consciousness, then off and on throughout the day. But do you know when I cried the least? When I was holding Aiden. When he was in my arms, his precious little face turned up toward mine, I cried the least. I could see it in his eyes, even though they couldn't focus on me yet. "Everything is going to be okay, Mama. Everything is going to be okay."

What lessons of love and life and acceptance this amazing boy has taught me. He is two years old as I write this book, and I feel lucky for every day I get to be with him. He has taught me, in a real, tangible way, a bit of wisdom his father has been telling me for years: "See the perfection."

Aaron has said that to me since I met him, often at difficult times, but even during joyous ones. "See the perfection." He taught me to see the perfection in the painful experiences we had earlier in our lives—they brought us to each other. When we don't have any money to go out, he reminds me how great it will be to stay home and make fun of television in bed. When we don't have money to take the kids on a vacation, he reminds me we do have money to buy them new back-to-school clothes and put a little in a savings account for a rainy day fund. When it starts "raining" later in the year and we owe unexpected medical bills, he reminds me that we can pay them because we have a little savings. Amazing man. See the perfection.

"See the perfection" is another way of saying, "It's all good." The change comes. It stirs things up, or in the extreme, it rocks our worlds. We cannot avoid it. No one gets out of this life without challenge and loss and change. Did we really think we could avoid it? I think part of our pain may come from the false belief that we can avoid change, that if we live well enough, we'll sneak by without suffering, and that if unwanted change does happen, it's a direct result of our having done something wrong. We attach so much judgment to change. We believe that the loss or the diagnosis or the change is bad. But is it? Is it really?

"A good marriage is one which allows for change and growth in the individuals and in the way they express their love."
PEARL S. BUCK

I am reminded of a story that feels like a fable I heard years ago. I don't remember it well, but it was of a man who, at the age of eighteen, was in a horrible accident and lost his leg. Everyone mourned. Then the draft for the war came along and, because of his lost leg, he couldn't serve. Many of the young men in the town who were drafted and able to serve were killed in the war. So, as the story goes, the loss of his leg saved his life. It's all in your perspective.

Is the change good or bad? It depends on how you look at it. And perhaps beyond that, do we need to label it one or the other? Could we not just look at the change as different? Ah, this is different. Didn't see this coming. Hmm. This will present some unique challenges. There will be the chance to grow, to learn, to open my heart. There may be the chance to teach others, to inspire, to love in unexpected ways. I have no idea how I'm going to handle this.

Roll with the Changes

I have a suggestion on how to roll with even the most rocking of changes. I think of the process in three steps.

Each one is key. Don't skip ahead.

First, there will be mourning of the loss of the status quo. We will mourn the loss of our body's ability, our health, the absence of pain. We will mourn the loss of our dream for our child, our dream of her having a perfectly healthy body and a long and pain-free life. We will mourn and weep and feel the loss in our bones. We'll mourn whatever the change is until we're done.

I have been counseled in my life to "live in the tension," and I think there is wisdom there. When something major shifts or changes in your life, when something cherished is lost, it is painful. Live in that discomfort for a time. Our instinct is to try to get out of the pain as quickly as possible, put a salve on it, take a pill, shake it off. But the discomfort will whisper pearls of wisdom, pearls you will most definitely miss if you brush the pain under the rug too quickly. I know there will be the urge to resist this part. You just want to get on with it, move ahead already. What's your problem? Life's not perfect. Nobody ever promised you a rose garden. But don't dismiss this pain and sense of loss so quickly. Allow it to shake you to your core. You're strong enough to take it.

> Steps to embracing a profound change:
>
> 1. Mourn
> 2. Examine with gratitude what remains
> 3. Look for ways to grow

Then, when you come to a place of peace after whatever the mourning looks like for you, look at what remains. Who else are you other than someone with a diagnosis or other change? When we're done mourning, we can celebrate what remains. For my son, I celebrate every day he puts anything in his mouth. He put a cookie in his mouth! He didn't bite it, but he put it in there. This is a cause for celebration. I celebrate his sounds and his ability to walk, and I don't focus on the fact that other boys his age are talking and eating up a storm.

My friend Cinda is a gifted child therapist. Years ago, she

taught me a ceremony that has been a blessing in my life. With her permission, I share it with you now. She calls it a "candle ceremony." Many of you may be familiar with some form of this ritual, but perhaps it's also new to some.

To accept a profound change, you light a single candle (I suggest using those little tea candles because you'll need ten or twenty by the time you're done). The single candle represents what is lost—health, ability, a dream. Around that candle, place and light additional candles. Each candle around the center one represents what remains.

With Aiden I may light a candle for his ability to see, to walk, to hug me, to roll over. Each ability he has that I can think of celebrating with the lighting of a candle is worth including. Don't second-guess yourself ("Well, I'm not sure if a smile qualifies . . ."). Just light the candle. Place each one into the circle until you have a ring of light surrounding the single candle of mourning in the middle.

Now, carefully extinguish the center candle. Put out its light to symbolize that ability, that specific dream, leaving your life. And then sit. Sit and take in the continued light from the remaining candles. Marvel at how much light is still left in your life. You'll recognize that, yes, without the center candle, the overall light is different. But then you'll take in the full measure of the ring of light that still burns bright. Sit there, taking it in, staring openly to let the firelight dance in your eyes. Close your eyes. Feel the warmth of the light and the warmth of what remains.

I would like to say something here about the power of ritual in my life. I do not claim to be an expert in this area, and I am sure there are others who could speak with more authority on the subject, but here is one woman's perspective. Years ago, I did not place any value on ritual, or at least not consciously. I think I even looked with some judgment at people who would carry or wear or employ what looked like talismans to me. I do not have judgment about any of those things now. Rituals can ground you to the earth when pain or loss or other powerful changes want to carry you off and away. I have found that creating a ritual around love or a relationship or even loss puts ground under my feet where before there was none.

These small rituals are not elaborate things, although they could be. There aren't always candles involved. Sometimes there's no physical object. Sometimes it's just going to the same place on the same day. It may be the ritual of walking the same ground, being in the same space, feeling the wind in the same trees. For instance, I drive past the building where I used to practice law whenever I need to feel grateful for the job I have today. With no disrespect intended to the law firm, my spirit felt trapped there, and when I drive past that building, I remember the feeling of driving into the parking garage, down, down, down below the sun. And in the depths of my heart, doing this cures me of whatever small resentment I might feel toward my current job. Sometimes my ritual is just wearing the ring my mother gave me, twirling it around on my finger and remembering her sweet face, or making her chocolate cake recipe and watching my family enjoy it, scraping the plates with their forks.

> What are some rituals you could add to your life to give you comfort and courage in facing profound change? Could you create a ritual around letting go of a role you cherished? Could you create a ritual around welcoming a new role into your life, like grandmother or empty-nest mother?

Okay. On to part three of embracing profound change. After you've mourned and you've examined what remains, it's time to grow. Let's get curious about what this change means for us and our hearts.

We wouldn't have chosen the change—that goes without saying. But here it is. What do we do with it now? Since the change of something major puts you in a place of near total confusion anyway, you might as well shake it up some more. Everything feels so strange and unusual—why not make it a little more strange and unusual? (I already vote for putting a little more "strange and unusual" into everyday life anyway.)

It's like the way you feel when you have a new job. The

whole thing feels so different—the drive to work, the people you work with, the tasks you perform, the whole vibe of the thing. What's getting your hair cut then? There's already so much change going on, what's a little more?

Think for a minute. Perhaps you're not as healthy as you used to be. You may be limited in what you are able to do or the time you have to do it in. Who are you now? Who is the you remaining beneath this penetrating change? What does *this* new you want to do? There may be roles that will fall away, roles that seem unnecessary and meaningless now. There may be new roles added in their place. You may teach someone, a daughter, a neighbor, how to live with challenges by the way you live. You may learn yourself even as you teach. Don't analyze the thoughts that come to your mind. Don't worry about it too much. The new you may want to call and volunteer. Extend yourself. You'll never regret it. It's not possible to regret extending yourself in love.

My mother used to say that kind of thing to me when I was little and acting in a selfish way. While ironing, and not looking at me throwing a tantrum across the room, she'd say almost under her breath, "I think someone needs to go to the hospital and donate some of her time to someone less fortunate."

That would make me crazy. Arrrggghhh! But she was right, of course. If I felt lost and cramped and resentful, the best way to work the cramp out was to love someone else, to give of myself to someone. And it's still true, perhaps even more so in my adult life than in my childhood. When I feel sorry for myself or for my children, wrapped up in what's missing and never will be, I need to give. I need to give of my time and my energy, of whatever I have to offer.

After we receive a diagnosis that limits us, how do we break through those limitations? We run for the cure. We sponsor someone else who can run for the cure. We donate our time or our money or our ability to a cause. We show our children or parents or coworkers how to live with joy after a loss. We roll with the changes.

CHAPTER FIVE

"Who Am I Without Her?"

As I write these words, it is the three-month anniversary of my mother's death. She was not a young woman when she died, and she had suffered mightily in the years before her passing. She had led a full life. Isn't that what they say? She was a devoted wife in the fullest sense of the phrase, and the kind of mother who would gladly give up her afternoons and her stashed away money and anything else for her children.

In the last months, she was ready to go. She warned me a few weeks before she died, "You have to let me go, Amanda."

"I know, Mama," is all I could muster in reply. I suppose those facts should add up to my being glad to let her go, or if not glad, at least ready. Many people who cared for me told me at the time that it was "for the best," and they may have been right, but not for my best. At least that's the way it felt.

My mother was my rock. She was the soft voice on the other end of the phone that would tell it like it is, however unflattering. "Amanda, you're too old to be having babies."

Yeah, I know, Mom, but I am.

"Oh, Amanda, why would you spend all those years in law school if you didn't want to be a lawyer?"

I don't know, Mom. It seemed like a good idea at the time.

"It's not going to be easy to lose all that weight at your age, Amanda."

I know, Mom. Pass the peanut butter.

My mother had the sweetest singing voice, high and smooth like the actresses who played angels in movies made in the forties. She had the prettiest face. Her features were just . . . perfect. Full lips, arched brows, high cheekbones, soft, chestnut hair that she wore back in a ponytail until she was past sixty. She was a real beauty, the kind of woman both men and women alike admire. My mother was a great baker, too, an inspired quilter, and a patient needlepointer. She knew what she knew, this woman who grew up next-to-next-to-youngest in a family of fourteen, with parents who forgot to feed her and stole her bus ticket so they could go to work.

However poor her upbringing, my mother's adult life was rich, not only because of what my father provided, but because of what she sought out. Her life was filled with flowers and hummingbirds and friends. My mother would keep a friend for seventy years.

I had feared her loss for many years before I actually lost her. I'm sure that says something about a weakness in me, but this is a change I dreaded. When it finally came, when I sat down beside her in that hospital room in Pennsylvania, and she recognized me for the last time, I was filled with love. She looked up at me with her round eyes so animated and said in a cherubic voice, "Oh, Amanda, it's you!" We hugged and held hands. I fed her cereal for breakfast and a couple of bites of toast. And an hour later, she closed her eyes.

She opened both her eyes and mouth one more time many hours later when a nurse tried to force her to take her medication. This wonderful nurse, an avid Penn State fan whose smock was adorned with Nittany Lion memorabilia, got up on the bed with real authority and told my mother she was going to take her medication one way or the other. My mother's tired eyes flashed open, and she said with all the strength her voice had mustered so often in my youth, "Oh, shut up!"

Those were the last words she ever said.

Who am I now that my mother is gone? I am still her daughter. I catch myself still doing things to please her, to make her proud of me. I put on the jewelry she gave me that she liked to see me wear, and I have the thought, *Mama would be so glad I remembered to wear this.* I bake her choco-late chip cookies, and when they turn out a little crunchy, I hear her saying, "You used too much butter." I think of her sit-ting beside me sometimes on a late Sunday afternoon when the sun has gone down, and I stop the TV on an old Katharine Hepburn movie just for a second. I feel like an or-phan without my mother, a forty-five-year-old orphan. And the world is my orphanage.[1]

At some point in our lives, we all lose someone, someone we think we cannot live without. This is a change that comes to each of us. We lose our parents, our friends, our spouses, even our children. I heard it said once that when you lose a parent, you become an orphan. When you lose a spouse, you become a widow. But when you lose a child, it is such a ter-rible occurrence that there is no word for it. There is no word for a loss on that scale.

I know there is no making this kind of change easy, or even easier. I will not try to talk the pain out of that kind of loss. I don't believe it's possible or even helpful. What I will suggest is for any of you in that situation to feel the pain for exactly as long as you need to feel it, whether it's minutes or

---

1. I heard this wonderful analogy—that the world is our orphanage—on a tape col-lection from psychologist Marianne Woodward.

years, knowing all the while that this loss you feel connects you to the human family.

Maya Angelou said of the great Thomas Wolfe novel *You Can't Go Home Again* that she liked the book, but disagreed with the title. You can never *leave* home, was Ms. Angelou's point. You are always home, no matter where you are, no matter with whom. Yes, I agree. I felt at home with my mother when I read those comments. I felt connected to her, as I feel connected to all daughters who have lost their mothers. Suddenly, I am a member of this sacred group, this club of orphaned daughters. I see it in their eyes when they hug me. They know. They know why there are tears so near the corners of my eyes, and they love me for it. I lost my mother and became a member of a group of people who love me not for anything I do or accomplish or give the world—only that I live without her.

My four-year-old son Ethan wondered why I was crying the other day. "I miss Grandma," I said, wiping away tears. His eyes went big. "It's okay, Mama. You have me!" Yes. We all go through this change of letting go of the hand of one family member to reach for the hand of another. We grow up in one family, dependent on our parents and grandparents, aunts and uncles, people we believe will always be there. And then as we mature, we slowly let go of that family and cling to the new one we've created—a spouse, children, friends, and coworkers who depend on us, people we believe will always be there.

We don't feel the change. It happens so subtly, until death. With death we have to let go, at least physically—remove her rings, take off her watch, and squeeze the hands of our new family a little harder.

When We Have No Choice

Sometimes change leaves us no choice. Our loved one dies. And with her or him, a part of us dies. Maybe our heart dies. Maybe our hope for chance of reconciliation dies. At least that's how it feels. How do we keep going? How do we wake up and make the children breakfast, take them to school, put gas in the car? We have no alternative.

We meet the change we thought we could not endure with whatever strength we can muster. We overwork or overeat or we go nights and nights without sleep. We hover over our children or don't spend enough time with them to hide our suffering. We handle the change the best way we can—that's how we do it—and those of you who have been through this loss know exactly what I'm talking about and could teach us all something about change when you have no choice. We honor our lost loved one by loving the living. That's what we do. We hug the children, the neighbors, the relatives, and we let them hug us back. We love the living.

When you lose the person you think you cannot live with-out, what specific changes do you experience? You may sleep on their side of the bed. You may buy different food at the grocery store. He never liked pota-toes, so you always served rice, but now that he's gone you eat baked potatoes every night. You behave differently financially. Once you fig-ure out which bank he kept the money in, you move it to an entirely new one, one you've driven by for years that you always thought looked nice. You sell his car and drive something new. You sell his house and live somewhere new. Change may permeate everything you do without him. And for you, it may feel like the more change, the better.

We honor our lost loved one by loving the living. That's what we do.

But the opposite may be true. You may need to do things exactly the same for a time, because you can't handle any more change. You need something, anything, to stay still, to not move, not change. You may serve dinner at exactly the same time she liked it, leave her chair empty, watch the same TV shows she used to like, even if you don't really care for them. You may go on taking care of the children just the way she always did. It may even occur to you that you feel guilty that you don't notice her absence as much as you thought you would. Until night comes, of course. Or until the smell of an old sweater of hers nearly knocks you out with grief.

No matter what works for you, the answer is—you cope. That's what you do. You cope with the change because you have no choice in the matter. I think about the change discussed in the last chapter that comes with the loss of health. Perhaps the candle ceremony we talked about there would be helpful here, lighting a candle for the person who is gone and then one for everyone who remains. Because that's the point: you cope and carry on because life is for the living. You keep making the children breakfast and keep driving to work because that's what you have to do. You try not to judge how well or not well you're doing it. You just keep on keeping on. If any kind of ceremony will help you, any kind of ritual, then do it. If keeping her clothes or getting rid of them immediately will help you, then do it.

When someone is gone, who remains? Who are the people who still need your love and attention? Write down their names, picture their faces, think about something you could do for each one of them that shows them how much you love them, however imperfectly. Begin with something small—a hug, a cupcake, a ride to the burger joint. Love the living!

There is no right way or wrong way, no right or wrong length of time. Don't worry about what anybody else thinks but you. This is your loss, your challenge, your change. They can deal with their own change in their own way when it's their turn. And while I know that your life will never be the same without her, it will be okay.

Everything will be okay.

It Was a Special Time

When we reflect back on funerals, on the days we held hands all the time without talking, on going through belongings and reminiscing about the way she looked in this necklace or the books he loved, we often describe those days as "a special time." How can that be? How can a time so filled with pain and loss be "special"?

Let's pause for a moment and really think about this question because there is magic in the answer.

It takes time. Don't expect to think of your wife's funeral as "special" for many, many months or possibly even years. But at some point, you might. You might just remember how very loved you felt during those sad days. You didn't know before that day how much your wife's family loved *you*—not just their daughter. Not just their grandchildren. You. Perhaps you didn't know how much your children admired you, how much they honored you, how they wanted only your happiness. You may never have known the depth of their love without this loss. And these tender disclosures were special.

I have a dear friend named Carol who lost her husband on the day before her son's wedding. Her husband died in his early fifties of a heart attack, so young, so utterly unexpected. She had no time to mourn him before she had to put on her dress and go to the wedding reception, where no one had time to learn of his death, so all night long, people kept asking where her husband was. She kept accepting hugs, kept smiling at her beautiful children on what she hoped would somehow still be a special day for them.

Later that week, after the funeral, when her friends and family gathered in her backyard to eat casseroles and visit, she stood on the back patio and leaned against the door, listening to people laughing and telling stories about her husband. She had never felt so alone in the world. She thought, *I don't know how to take care of myself. I can take care of the kids, but not myself. How will I do that without him?*

That moment was nearly thirty years ago, and while Carol would never show pride in anything she's done, I can tell you she's managed incredibly well. I'm sure she would have rather had her husband with her all this time, sharing the burdens of life, helping her figure out how to counsel her children, but she's found her way in the world, and it's been a beautiful way, a way filled with service to others. She may even look back on those days, the insanity of a funeral and a wedding so close together, and tell you that it was a "special time."

For my own part, I recall the days my rock of a brother, Dave, his beautiful wife, Deirdre, and my loving sister, Connie, and I spent in my mother's hospital room before she died. We had a slumber party there for three days while her breathing slowed and finally stopped. The nurses brought us reclining chairs and extra pillows. Deirdre got us take-out and slices of pie. We ate them—or tried to eat them—and showered in the nurses' lounge. Sometimes we laughed. Often we cried. One evening, my father slept in the bed next to my mother's, and they both looked so peaceful. If I hadn't known she was dying, I would have thought they were both just dozing with a football game on in the background, as they so often did in my memories of childhood weekends— soft snoring with an official announcing from the field "penalty will be assessed on the kickoff." One of us kids wondered out loud while they slept why mom was still hanging on, and Deirdre said, "She's probably having too much fun watching and listening to us."

> Think of three special times in your life that were also painful. Hold each one in your heart for just a moment and remember the gifts it gave you.

That, yes that, was a special time.

I'm not saying you have to *do* anything. You don't have to let go of the pain or the loss or the grief. You don't have to try to replace it with anything. You don't have to move on or get up or get over it. I'm just telling you that it's going to be okay. You may not see that yet, and you don't need to. But it's still true, and it has been since the beginning of time.

CHAPTER SIX

"Oh! If You Had Seen Me Then!"

I have never met a woman who was happy with her figure. I suppose one exists, but I've never met her. Every woman of every size I've ever known has said something like, "Ya know, it's my stomach. I just can't get rid of this roll on my stomach. See?" and she grabs a big handful to make the point.

Thank you for sharing.

Or maybe she says, "I'm fine with everything but the arms. See this part right here underneath? It's like a sub-arm. I have an arm, and a sub-arm." Yes, I see that. Now.

Or she says, "I never wear shorts anymore. I'm not over-weight, really. It's the cottage cheese thing," and she shudders just at the thought of it.

I believe men have their insecurities, too, with their changing and aging bodies, but they just don't talk about them as much as women do, at least not to me. We women, though—we feel the need to express ourselves to anyone who will listen, and always to someone who will compliment us. If a coworker stops you in the hall to say, "You look fantastic in that dress," what do you say? "Yeah. It hides my big hips!"

This is the million-dollar question. Literally. How can we embrace the natural changes of our aging bodies? Truly embrace them, with love and openness and freedom? As a group, women spend millions—even billions—of dollars trying to reverse the aging process with surgery and Botox and every other imaginable thing. We spend money we don't have on procedures we don't need.

We want the way we feel when we think we're beautiful. That's what we're searching for.

And why? It's not that we actually need a differently shaped nose. We won't be the ones looking at it most of the time. We want the way we *feel* when we think we're beautiful. That's what we're searching for. If we could feel beautiful, not the we're-talking-ourselves-into-it-when-we-know-better beautiful, but if we genuinely felt beautiful, we wouldn't want or need to alter anything. Trying to *get* beautiful is a means to the end of *feeling* beautiful.

It's the feeling we're after.

In many of our minds, the feeling can come only when our estimation is confirmed by others. It's not enough for us to think we might be beautiful. We don't trust our own judgment. We're not sure we even have our own judgment. That's why we try to look like movie stars. If we can have Angelina Jolie's lips and Brad Pitt's abs, then we must be beautiful. Everyone agrees that they are beautiful. The rest is simple scientific method. If they are beautiful and I equal them, then I am beautiful. We think this will bring us acceptance. This will bring us approving looks from women at lunch and men standing in the movie line. And why do we want those admiring looks? Because of the way they make us *feel*.

> Think of three times when you felt truly beautiful. Where were you? Who were you with? What made you feel beautiful in those moments?

The Makeover

We've all seen the makeover shows on TV where they pull a mother of three off the street and turn her into a glamorous woman. Her "before" picture shows messy hair, possibly still with baby food in it, no makeup, and an untucked shirt over baggy jeans. And she's not accessorized!

Her "after" picture shows coiffed hair with dazzling makeup, perfectly unwrinkled clothes and stylish shoes. (The shoes are always great on makeovers, aren't they?) When she walks out in front of the audience, newly transformed, we at home do the same thing everyone does who's there in person—we gasp. We catch our breath at the vision of this woman so changed. The woman beams with the approval of so many people, especially her husband or children, who are seated down front. She sees how beautiful she is in their eyes, in the applause of the audience, and she trusts that, at least for the moment, it's true.

There is something to learn from the makeover concept. Why does it prompt the subject to appear to feel better? Why does it make us in the audience feel better? It's the energy! There is energy in feeling revived, renewed, re-polished. In some cases, other than the lipstick, it's hard to tell which is the "before" and which is the "after." She might not really look much different afterward. What gives it away is the energy. And the energy comes from two places: (1) the change and (2) the feeling of attractiveness. We already know change brings a charge—any change—different color, different hair, different boots. It all brings energy with it. That's part of what this book is about.

But what about the feeling of attractiveness and the energy that comes with that? The *feeling* of beauty and acceptance is a powerful, distinct thing, so elusive, so separate from the energy of the change itself. You can have change without the feeling of beauty. You can have beauty without the change. And remember—when it comes to beauty—it's the feeling we seek, not the fact of it.

I imagine many of these women go home, wash the makeup off, and go back to being the same woman they've always been. Is there anything wrong with that? Is there any part of you who read that and thought, "Ah, that's too bad." There is something in us that believes women ought to do everything they can to look attractive. We are brought up to believe that a woman should keep up her appearance. We hear the language, "She's really let herself go." Go where? Go "to pot"? To town? To the local dessert bar?

In any given week, I'm sure there are times when, if other people could see us, they would say we have really let ourselves go. (For me, that would be last Saturday afternoon around 4:00 when I still hadn't showered or gotten dressed and was trying to bake a carrot cake.) I'm trying to figure out where the line is between taking care of these heavenly bodies we've been given, honoring the blessing that is life by caring for our health, and obsessing about looking a certain way. The answer is hiding in the feeling.

Some preliminary questions: If you let yourself go over 150, 175, 200 pounds, do you cry? Do you count yourself a failure? Do you feel unlovable? Do you feel like you should try to lose weight because that's better for your health?

Because your kids would be proud of you? Because you'd feel more accepted in general?

For men, if you begin to lose your hair, do you feel less masculine? Less attractive to your mate? What if your wife told you—and meant it—that your hair didn't matter to her in the least? Would that fix the way you feel, or would you still feel "less" somehow? Stay with me now. Some answers are forthcoming.

We all know people who are beautiful but don't know it. A woman may look like Gwyneth Paltrow, but truly doesn't believe it. All she sees is large hands, big feet, and a flat chest. That's how she defines herself. The triple threat. When people compliment her, she thinks the other person is just being polite, like you are when you tell a little girl she looks beautiful in her mother's hat and makeup. *Feeling* beautiful has so much less to do with actually *being* beautiful than we might think. Yes, you can have the makeover. You can have the extreme makeover. Some of your friends and neighbors may notice you've done something, but not all of them will think it's for the good.

Feeling beautiful has so much less to do with actually being beautiful than we might think.

"Did you see Alice? What is wrong with her face?" If you lose weight, many people will be happy for you, either because you look great or because they want you to be healthy, but what if you're losing weight because you have an illness that prevents you from maintaining your body weight? Should your friends be happy for you then? Will you *feel* beautiful then? I am reminded of a line from a popular movie when the girl who is trying to make it in the fashion industry says, "I'm just one good stomach flu away from my goal weight." Every woman in that audience got it. Been there. Felt that.

The Way You Make Me Feel

What makes us feel beautiful, at eighteen, at thirty-five, at fifty, or eighty? Another person. In my way of thinking, it takes another person to make us feel beautiful. Beauty is a relationship feeling. If we live a secluded life for whatever reason, we might feel fine and good and happy, but not often *beautiful* without a mirror—a human mirror. So, knowing that, how do we achieve the feeling of beauty while also embracing the natural change of our bodies as we age? In order to answer that primary question, we need to know where the mirror is pointed.

When we are young, we need people to look *at* us to feel beautiful. We need other boys and girls, people in general, to look at us. Stare, if possible. We wear clothes and style our hair and drive cars and play music, all to get their attention.

The more attention, the better. And when they're looking at us, on some level, we feel beautiful in their eyes.

You see this in toddlers, "Look at me, Mommy! Watch me! Watch me!" The dive in the pool or the twirl in the full skirt doesn't make them feel as good without eyes on them. Perhaps this is why teenagers act out when they don't get sufficient attention from their parents and peers. They need a mirror, any mirror, in order to feel beautiful, to feel anything.

This kind of feeling of beauty is not limited to children. My mother was a beautiful woman, so beautiful in her youth that it was very difficult for her to experience aging and then sickness—kidney disease—which she saw as detracting from her beauty. If you complimented her, she would brush it off and talk about how awful she looked. She would explain to us regularly that if it weren't for those darn steroids she had to take, she could lose some weight and get her figure back.

It wasn't until the last years of her life that I saw the shift in her understanding of beauty. In the final year of her life,

---

Think of five people whom the sight of makes you feel beautiful. And remember, this is about the way you feel when you look *at* them. For me they would include

my husband
my children
my sweet father
my brother and his beautiful wife
my sister and her beautiful family

she felt beautiful every time she looked at my youngest son, Aiden. I took him to see her in Pennsylvania as often as I could during those days. She would hold him, give him a bottle, admire him trying to stand up next to a chair, and in those moments she felt genuinely beautiful. The size of her skirt, the wrinkling or bruising of her skin didn't matter at all. The feeling of absolute beauty came from looking *at him*.

This is the "aha" moment. The way to feel beautiful at any age, with any body, is to shift the focus. We no longer need people to look *at us* to feel beautiful—we need to look *at people*. We become the mirror for them.

Real beauty is the end of needing to be seen, and the beginning of seeing.

Beauty, real beauty, truly is in the eyes of the beholder and not the "beheld." The beholder feels beautiful herself because she loves what she beholds.

When our toddlers throw their arms up into the air for us to scoop them up, we feel beautiful. When our wives run to greet us after we return home from a trip, we feel beautiful. When our children get married and tell us they're expecting their first child, we feel beautiful. None of those feelings requires that we look any certain way for other people to admire. We can be thin or heavy, wrinkled or smooth, tan or pale, weak or strong. We can "let ourselves go" or stay in perfect shape. We can be exactly the way we are right now at this moment . . . and we can be the way we'll be in five years and twenty years and beyond. We can age without any concern for stretching our face until it feels smooth. The feeling of beauty requires only that we look at the objects of our love and devotion.

This is finally it—the end of needing to be seen, and the beginning of seeing.

CHAPTER SEVEN

"I Don't Know What Else to Do!"

You walk in the door to work, feeling the same way you've felt for the last twenty-four years of doing the same thing. You're just turning on your computer and settling in when your supervisor approaches and asks to see you in her office. You walk down the hall, feeling no specific trepidation, until you reach the doorway and see the director of human resources sitting in the chair next to the one you sit in. You've believed for a long time that you are the most productive person in your department, the star of your team. You've worried about losing your job from time to time, just like the next guy, but only in the abstract because, really, who would fire you? No one has approached you about a pay cut or anything, but now they inform you that you are losing your job. When you push for a reason, all they say under direction of their lawyers is that "the company is going in a different direction."

You're numb. You sit dumbfounded, not wanting to get up, because surely there's *something* you can do. Don't they realize what you've given to this company? They'll have to hire three people to replace you! The HR director starts describing what your severance package will look like—three months' pay. You don't know if that's good or bad, but you're grateful for it. When you have no other questions, they tell you that it's company policy that you pack up and leave the premises immediately. They escort you back to your desk, where there are moving boxes propped up against your cubicle. How did those get there? You pack up the picture of your family, your old Franklin Planners, and some books you think belong to you and not the company. Coworkers avoid your eyes, except for the brave ones who come to shake your hand, pat you on the shoulder, and say they're really going to miss you. The security guard walks you to your car. What? Were they afraid you'd steal some paperclips on the way out?

Change can happen in an instant.

One minute you describe yourself as a lawyer or an account manager or a customer service representative, and the next minute you don't. Now who are you? Where is your value? You had thought your value was in your work, in that work, in that job. That's why you gave it 110 percent for so many years. That's why you were more loyal to it than to your family or friends sometimes—something you've often felt guilty about and now deeply regret. That job was who you were, the sum of your contribution, the biggest part of your life, or so you thought. Now that the job is gone—what are you worth?

> "If you want to make enemies, try to change something."
> WOODROW WILSON

This is a question we all have to answer eventually, whether it's losing our job outside the home or losing our job when the children grow up and move on. I suggest you answer it sooner, without waiting for the downsizing, or natural and chosen retirement, but most of us don't. Most of us need the pain, the nudge of not knowing what to do next, to force us to find our true value.

What Do You Do All Day?

There was a time years ago when I was an attorney when I asked myself, "What is the heart of what I do all day?" I felt frustrated—soul-level frustrated—and I wanted to understand why. My father is a lawyer, a fine and trusted counselor, who inspired me when I was growing up with his stories of helping neighbors resolve their difficult situations. I wanted to be like him. I wanted to be smart enough to read those big, thick books with the terribly fine print, to help other people like he did. I can say in hindsight that I enjoyed law school, at least part of me did. I enjoyed the adventure of finding ways to make an argument. We'd be given a description of challenging circumstances with a single assignment—make an argument. How thrilling! Then came the actual practice of law, with real people involved who needed someone to make something happen. That's when I started to feel pain, and only then did I examine—what *did* I do all day?

When I realized the answer, my heart broke, and a decision was born in me. The answer was: I looked for things I could exploit. I looked for something you said or did or insinuated, and then I found a way to use it against you for my client's benefit. That's what I did all day. The title of lawyer was one I cherished, at least the thought of it, however briefly. I spent many years and endured more frustrations than some on my way to earning the business card with my name printed above "attorney at law." But it didn't take me long to realize that the title did not give me sufficient joy to be worthy of my precious life's blood. (Which is not to say that it doesn't for many, many great and effective counselors. I just didn't have what it took.)

Leaving the law firm was the most difficult and unsettling decision of my life. Who was I now? What was I now that my life's dream was over? What could I possibly do instead?

I think this is a question many of us ask: "What else could I do?" You can't think of another job, another profession, another viable endeavor that would earn a living for you and your family. Allow me to suggest that just because you can't think of one doesn't mean there isn't one. You haven't needed to think of one before now. You've always had a job, perhaps even the same job, for years. You've been good at it, and hopefully you've even enjoyed it for much of that time. But the times . . . they are a changin'. You feel a shift at work, in your heart, that may lead to a job change for you.

Just because you can't think of another job doesn't mean there isn't one.

What will that change look like? It may be finding a job at another company just like the one you do now. If you were a lawyer before, you could get a job as a lawyer at another firm. Perhaps you'd need to move, change cities, to stay in the same field you've always known. But what if what you do is very specialized? You might not be able to find another job that looks exactly like the one you're used to.

Let's go underneath the job description. What do you actually do? Do you use computer software? Do you write? Do you sell something? We all do that on some level. Do you interview people? Do you quickly learn new technologies? What do you actually do during your day?

I am a radio announcer at present, a job I absolutely love

and will do for as long as they'll have me. What do I actually do all day?

I talk. I talk for a living. I talk to people, about people, with people. I ask questions, offer opinions, interact. I am curious. If I had to write my job description using a single word, it would be, curiosity.

> What do you actually do all day? Break down the tasks, the activities, and the skills you use during your work day and see what they look like. There may be a message in there for you.

No one can do my job, at least not well and for long, without powerful curiosity in nearly all subjects. So if I got fired today and had to find another job, would I look in radio? Probably. Certainly. But what if a job in radio was not forthcoming? What else could I do?

I'd look into other forms of media: television, Internet, blogging. Perhaps I could be a public information officer for a company or governmental entity. Maybe I could produce a show for another host. Maybe I could teach, something I have done and enjoyed thoroughly. I could write books (oh, wait—already doing that). Maybe I could work as a press secretary for an elected official, or I could be a spokesperson for a celebrity or even for a nonprofit organization. And these are just the jobs I've thought of in the last two minutes. I am sure there are a dozen more

I haven't considered, but could if I began to apply real energy to the challenge.

I hear some of you already in the back of my ear, "Sure, Amanda. It's easy for you to say. You've had so many jobs." True. I've had eighteen jobs in my coming-up-on-fifty years, and I've been good at four or five of them. But even if you graduated from high school and got a job at the factory and have been there ever since, let's take a look at it. I know many auto workers and others who are in this exact position. They've made good money making cars for twenty years, and suddenly that model isn't selling anymore, and they truly feel like that's all they know how to do.

> What else could you do? If you lost your job today, make a list of all the other jobs you can think of that you might enjoy and think you could be qualified for. Don't hold yourself back. There is a lot you can do.

Okay—come with me. What do you *really* do for a living? You assemble things. You follow instructions. You pay attention to detail. You work as a team. You work with tools, sometimes unwieldy tools, often new and different tools. You do what it takes to get the job done and done on a deadline. You take pride in your work. Maybe you manage other employees. Now, let's open our minds to what other jobs those skills might apply to. Putting aside the obvious ones, such as other factory jobs, could you learn how to work in a bakery or restaurant with all that attention to detail and following instructions? Could you assemble something else, something informational, something in technology? Could you use your experience with heavy machinery on a construction site? Could you use the determination you've developed to help an office—any office—that's struggling, a mortgage company, a real estate company, a software company? Is there something you've always wanted to learn? Well, now is the time to learn it!

I Never Would Have Thought

Many of the people I've interviewed over the years have said something like this to me, "I never would have thought I'd go into politics . . . or develop my own product . . . or be a stay-at-home parent . . . or build my own company from scratch." I know there are some people who get a dream when they're twelve (Bill Gates) and follow it through to amazing fruition, but most of us catch the waves that come at us.

I had no intention of becoming a radio announcer when I was a young woman. I simply met someone who said, "You know, Amanda, you've got a deep voice. You could make a living with that voice." Hmm. I had never considered that.

When you're facing a job change, you may want to go to those comments, the things people have complimented you on over the years, and see if there isn't a dream hiding in there somewhere.

My niece Amanda has always been good at doing other people's hair. She's done my hair and makeup every time we've been together since she was a teenager. She didn't take the talent seriously during much of her young life, because she was programmed to go to college (a dream I'm sure her Aunt Amanda contributed to). When she realized college wasn't for her, she remembered what she loved, what she was good at, and now she's off and running at a salon in South Carolina, and I am so proud of her.

> What have people complimented you on in your life? Do you have the best cookies, the most amazing backyard, a way with children? Are you a great speaker at church, the first person your friends want to call when they have a problem? What are you so good at that people want you to do it again?

It's true for all forms of change, including career change—the change we choose for ourselves is easier to stomach than the change that's chosen for us. I say *easier* because even that kind of change isn't easy.

My husband made a serious career change three years ago that was entirely his choice. He decided to leave his position as production director and became a full-time parent. When I got pregnant with our youngest son, we realized that our children needed a full-time parent. They needed one of us to be with them always, available to them, attending to them.

We knew it in our hearts, and we were struggling with how we would accomplish it, how we would afford it, when Aaron said, "I think it should be me."

I was a little shocked. "Really?"

"I would like it to be me if you feel comfortable with that," he offered humbly.

"Yes," I answered even before I was sure that was how I felt. "Yes. You're such an amazing father. I think that would be great, Honey, if you're sure you would be happy in that role."

He said he was as sure as anybody could be embarking on something entirely new and daunting. Two months later, he left the job he had loved for fifteen years.

The change was powerful, for all of us. Suddenly Aaron was living in this beautiful, timeless world where he didn't have to dress for work every morning or drive in rush hour traffic. On the flip side, suddenly he was living in a world where he was always on, 24/7, where he never had a day off or anywhere to go for adult conversation.

For the children, the change was immediate and visible. The kids had access to him throughout the day, even our teenagers, who I think benefited from his decision as much or more than the little boys. They felt loved, important, and more than a little surprised. They looked at life and work and career and family differently from that day forward. With his career change, Aaron felt like he now had the best clients he had ever had in his life—our five children—and he adores serving them. Aaron was an award-winning production director and producer during his career in radio, but he is an inspired father, and all of our lives work because of his choice to change.

Changing a job by choice can be a little like outgrowing a favorite, old pair of shoes. You love those shoes. They've been your friends for so long, but when they get too small or too uneven in their step, they get painful. They're squelching your feet. You just can't walk in them without discomfort. You've grown, and the old shoes can't grow with you.

Changing a job by choice can be a little like outgrowing a favorite, old pair of shoes.

When you find the new shoes, they are uncomfortable, to be sure, stiff and needing to be broken in. You don't know them, and they don't know you. But these are just growing pains, and you and the shoes will come to feel comfortable with each other before long. Take a walk. Show them the neighborhood.

Like Pulling Your Finger Out of Mud

In whatever work we choose, whether we are stay-at-home parents or CEOs, we want to feel needed, don't we? In our private thoughts, we sometimes feel like our business just wouldn't be the same without us, that things would fall apart without us. Of course, our better selves would never wish that on any company, especially not our family, but we don't want our contribution to go unnoticed. At least that's what I thought, until my mentor and friend Chris Redgrave taught me otherwise.

"When I leave this place, it will be like pulling your finger out of mud," she told me. "We'll eat some cake, have a hug, and you won't miss me the next day."

I couldn't believe it. Did she really mean that? Of course, it wasn't true, especially about the missing part. But I was flabbergasted at the unselfishness of it. And then I caught it—the vision of a leader so effective, so loyal to a company that she would ensure the company did not suffer even for a moment at the time of her exit.

What a wonderful metaphor for life that is—pulling your finger out of mud. We are here, we love and give and share and create, and when we're gone, other creative and passionate people come to take our place, filling the gap we left behind. They bring their ideas. They raise their families. If we are parents, our hope for our children is that they'll live their lives with vigor and integrity without us. We hope they'll get up in the morning and go to work and love their own children.

And isn't this exactly as it should be? Perhaps we spend too much time trying to make a mark, to be remembered. Let's forget about that, forget about our legacy and focus on our living.

CHAPTER EIGHT

"If You Never Change Your Mind, Why Have One?"

EDWARD DE BONO

I'd been angry with a certain woman for ten years. I was convinced that she did something to hurt me way back when. To protect the innocent, I won't go into the gory details but let me just say I felt wronged by her, seriously and most unfairly wronged. I never had 100 percent confirmation of this wrongdoing. We often don't, do we, of the grudges we hold so dear? We just think we know. We're pretty darned sure. And we blame them as if we're completely sure, but in the end—we're not 100 percent sure. But that didn't matter to me. What mattered was the way I felt whenever she walked into a room. I felt sick—so she must be guilty.

I hurt every time I saw that woman, which was quite regularly, but less so since. Even at the thought of seeing her

I felt a little sick to my stomach and broke out in hives along my jawline. I wondered how she felt about me.

She must know I know, I stewed. *How does she live with herself?* I judged.

As time passed and I saw her less often, I thought about the situation less—until recently, when I started to have interaction with her again. I found the feeling of resentment and blame gone, replaced by curiosity. Did that mean that I was never wronged in the first place? Was my 99.9 percent intuition incorrect? Or had time just healed all wounds? I was so convinced that she was a conniving, heartless, manipulating twit who was not to be trusted on any level, and yet—now, somehow I don't feel that way.

> "Change your thoughts, and you change your world."
> NORMAN VINCENT PEALE

Have I . . . could I have . . . is it possible that I have *changed my mind?*

Ahhhh. The absolute thrill of changing one's mind—about anything—but especially about the big things. In the end, perhaps those are the only changes that really matter.

We can change our circumstances, our environment, our relationships, our abilities, but if we don't change our minds, what are we left with? A reactive glob of uncertain insecurity, doomed to repeat old patterns in an attempt to learn lessons. Not pretty.

So how do we go about embracing a change of mind? How do we get past the criticism from others (or ourselves) that such a change would make us wishy-washy, uncommitted, faithless? I'm not sure I have the answer to this age-old question, but let's begin at the beginning.

New Information

We are presented with new information that conflicts with something we've believed to be true. Our judgment can only be as good as our information, right? In the example above, I had assumed, based on what I "knew" at the time and the "vibes" I got, that my former friend had wronged me. But then I received new information that that belief might not have been true.

Remember when we as a culture used to think that smoking cigarettes was *good* for you, or at least not bad? Our judgment was only as good as our information. As a human race, we once believed the world was flat, until we were presented with new, compelling information to the contrary. Some of our ancestors even believed that one race of people was superior to another because of the color of their skin, but now we have information that proves such a belief to be wholly without merit. Do we hold onto old beliefs out of respect for our grandparents or their grandparents? Of course not. As Abraham Lincoln said, "As our case is new, we must think and act anew."

How many of your beliefs do you claim out of long-standing habit or even out of loyalty to a parent or an elder?

> "We might as well require a man to wear still the coat which fitted him when a boy as civilized society to remain ever under the regimen of their barbarous ancestors."
>
> THOMAS JEFFERSON

How many beliefs do you hold onto because that's just the way it's always been done in your family?

Maybe in your family you've always thought of environmentalists as a "bunch of tree-huggers," but have you ever considered that some environmentalists might be kind and reasonable people who just want to care for the home they love, like you want to care for yours? Or maybe your family has always believed that young people, "if they have any sense," finish college before they get married and start having babies. But what if that's not true for everyone? What if marrying at eighteen and living happily together for sixty years is exactly what one couple is meant to do? Or perhaps you believe that any man worth his salt should be the breadwinner in his family, and that a "woman's place is in the home," but what if that isn't the best thing for a specific man, his wife, and his children? What if you've secretly (or not so secretly) resented the sound of Spanish being spoken in stores and school cafeterias, thinking "those people ought to learn to speak English," and then your son falls in love with a girl from Mexico, marries her, and starts speaking Spanish?

Hello. Welcome to the brave, new world.

We don't usually consider the possibility of our opinions being wrong until we're presented with new information that points us toward change, opens the door to a new way of thinking and lets us peek inside. We may not want to go in. We may weigh the choice and opt for maintaining the status quo, because we believe either that we are right to begin with or that we cannot face the psychic pain of a shift in thinking so profound. We may feel disloyal to a parent or a spouse or some unknown authority figure for even considering making such a mental shift.

But at least you peeked inside. Once you've done that, you are forever changed, if only a little bit. It's like the side street you've

Are there any beliefs passed down in your family that you might like to let go of? Were you taught that:

1. Boys matter more than girls and should be waited on hand and foot?
2. Yard work should be done by boys, inside work by girls?
3. Sports are for boys—girls should be more dainty?
4. What a girl weighs is more important than what she thinks?

Want to consider changing any of those beliefs, shake it up a little bit, see if something else might be true for *you*?

never driven before but have only glanced down at a stop-light. Looks like a nice street. *It would get me home just as fast, come to think of it. Maybe I'll just turn here and see what happens.* This is the beginning of change. You are flirting with becoming open-minded, and you know what that means.

It means you will never be invited on talk shows. Only people with very strong opinions on which there is no room for doubt and who will argue with anyone who disagrees with them to the death are invited on talk shows. Talk-show producers are specifically instructed to find people who will really "get into it" on the air, "go after each other," and "mix it up." (My inability to do any of those things is probably why I will likely never be a talk-show host.)

There is an exception to that rule, however. His name is Doug Wright, a talk-show host in Salt Lake City. Doug has been on the air for thirty years and has said for many of those years that the only people who really scare him are the people who can't change their minds. "Either they've achieved a state of enlightenment I can't imagine or they've stopped thinking altogether," Doug explained. (I'm going with the latter.) With Doug as the exception, I know an open mind doesn't often get good press.

Until now. The humility of an open mind is a beautiful and, may I say, a divine thing, not always easy to maintain in the face of strident assurances to the contrary, but beautiful nonetheless.

I am reminded of the lyrics of a U2 song where Bono sings, "I knew much more then than I do now."

I wondered when I first heard that song, *How could he know less now? Don't we learn more as we live? Don't we gain wisdom? Shouldn't I get smarter as I get older?* I pondered the lyrics, sat with the idea, then felt their meaning. There were things and beliefs I took for granted as a young person without exploring them, things that might not have been true.

The humility of an open mind is a beautiful and divine thing.

I'd thought I knew just about everything, who was good and who was bad, who was right and wrong, what mattered—more than my parents knew, at least. But with age and open-mindedness came humility. The older I get, the more I realize I have yet to learn. I "knew" much more then than I do now.

The Energy of an Open Mind

One of the unexpected pleasures of an open mind is the gift of energy that comes with it. I did not realize how much energy I expended, unconsciously in most cases, defending and maintaining the correctness of my opinions. I had to argue them, defend them, impose them on other people. I woke up stewing about them, wondering how I could convince other people of how right I was. Being right and staying right and then making sure everybody knows how right you are is exhausting work. You can't allow others to speak to the contrary in your presence. You can't hear them out. You begin to itch and flush and need to interrupt. You head for the chat room as soon as you get home to commiserate with others who see it your way.

The day you open your mind, even in a small way, to the possibility of changing the way you think, energy comes flooding in. You will be amazed at how much energy you were using to hold your opinions up in the air, like plates twirling on sticks, and how all of those rigid opinions were driving you slowly insane! Now that you can listen without anger, now that you can hear a contrary point of view, whether you change your mind or not, you will have much more energy for the other things you actually want to do in your life—like help your children with their homework. Have you ever had the experience of wanting to help your child with something, but you have to make them wait while you finish arguing with your wife first, telling her just how wrong she is and how right you are? When you're done, your spouse is deflated, you are exhausted, and your child long since got help on the Internet.

I am not suggesting you change any belief that is sacred to you or that you not defend such an opinion in the presence of a contrary one. I am speaking only of the natural consequences of living with an open mind. If I am Republican but open to a good idea from a Democrat, I will likely have more energy for jogging and making dinner than the Republican who has to refute the validity of any idea coming from across the aisle (and vice versa). If I believe that anyone without children is missing out on the most important experience in life and I go around trying to persuade all my single friends to marry, and then the married ones to have children or more children, I may be missing just how wonderful my friends are exactly as they are now and how much they are offering the world. I have found in my life that I can get lost in my own passions, my own convictions, my own good intentions, and only recently have discovered a remedy.

The remedy is listening.

With an open mind.

No one has ever been accused of listening too much. I read that somewhere recently, and it was a gift to my soul. I vowed that day to listen more, especially when I wanted to talk. I listen now to my coworkers when they're talking nonsense—I'm sorry—when they're expressing opinions I don't happen to agree with.

I listen to my husband every day no matter what the subject and especially when his voice drops down low. I listen to my teenagers and toddlers tell me about their day and what matters to them, asking follow-up questions when I don't understand what they meant. I listen to my father tell me on the phone about his table tennis matches this weekend and how his cooking for himself is coming along, asking about the brand of peas and carrots and the type of potato he's using.

> "Things do not change; we change."
>
> HENRY DAVID THOREAU

Listening lets me love so much more fully than talking does. Listening lets me hear what might be new information. Listening may lead to a change of thought. It may not, I realize, but it may. And in all of that blessed listening, I am freed from the need to impose myself and the rightness of my point of view.

Change Is a Solo Sport

We've got to come to this place ourselves, of course. Others may suggest, they may offer, they may inform us of a change we may want to consider. They might suggest we read books or listen to speakers or open our minds to their way of thinking. But then, at the end of all that, it is up to us and us alone to do it. Trying to force someone to change his mind— or even his brand of toothpaste—is like trying to force a toddler to take his medicine. The harder you try, the more resistant he is likely to be, until possibly he concedes, but without heart, without conviction. He has just reached the point when he'll do anything to get you to shut up.

Change is a solo sport.

Sometimes it's a sprint, sometimes a marathon, but it's always a solo endeavor. We may have coaches, supporters along the way who cheer us on, but at the moment of change, we are alone.

> "Those convinced against their will are of the same opinion still."
>
> DALE CARNEGIE

We are alone with the fear of who we'll be if we let go of an old, but deeply ingrained belief.

"But I've always felt that way," I hear you saying just before you let go. In a way, it's like saying good-bye to an old friend who tried to stab you in the back every time you turned around. This old friend didn't deserve you, didn't love you, but you'll miss him anyway. Such is the old belief, the old thought you'll let go of now. You may miss his familiar jibes, the usual judgments, but perhaps it is simply time to exchange the old gray shirt for a new orange sweater. You haven't worn it before, but that doesn't mean it won't be the one you get the most compliments on. Try it. Think differently about your neighbors, your parents, yourself. And watch the universe swirl at your feet.

CHAPTER NINE

There Is No Such Thing As a Habit You Don't Want

I used to be late for everything. Late to meet friends, late for staff meetings, late to the airport. I was a dillydallier. That was a phrase my mom used a lot when I was growing up. "Stop your dillydallying!" When I made it to college, I was regularly late to class, even on test days. I remember showing up to a law school exam twenty minutes late. What was I thinking, that I was so smart I could ace the test without needing all the allotted time? Noooooo. That definitely was not it. Being late, especially on that occasion, terrified me. I had a decidedly destructive, not to mention rude, habit.

I would try to excuse myself with self-deprecation. "Oh, I'm so sorry." (I said that a lot.) "I just can't seem to be on time to save my life! I am not to be trusted, not with your time, not with anything!" I would smile, make wild gestures of apology, hoping the enthusiasm of my *mea culpa* appeased them. Sometimes my friends or clients would accept these lame excuses.

Sometimes I felt the need to add detail. "The traffic was so much worse than I expected," or, "I overslept my alarm, the only piece of machinery less reliable than I am," or, "My mom called just as I was walking out the door, and I really needed to talk to her."

I offered detailed descriptions of what I had been doing that delayed me ten or twenty or even thirty minutes. And at the time, I genuinely thought those explanations were the reason for my tardiness. I thought *they* made me late.

Until I got a job in radio. One of the many wonderful things about this job is that it is completely unforgiving of tardiness. When the ABC news ends at four minutes and thirty seconds past every hour, you've got to be in the booth. If you're not in the booth, there will be dead air, and dead is the right adjective to describe what will happen if silence comes out of the speakers. Dead air is not tolerated for any reason in my industry. We don't even like pregnant pauses.

The fourth or fifth time I was "just a couple minutes late" to my air shift, my program director called me into his office and stated calmly, "This morning you were late."

I answered with my usual sincere exasperation. "Oh, yes, I'm sooooo sorry, Rod. I turned the alarm off when I thought

I had hit the snooze button and . . ." That was followed by nervous laughter. Mine, not his.

He replied, "The next time you're late, you don't work here anymore."

Dead air.

I have, with the rarest of exceptions, not been late to anything since that conversation more than ten years ago. The bluntness of it, the realization that I could lose something I thoroughly loved, motivated me to change my life. I accepted a truth I had been fighting for most of my life—that it wasn't the weather, the traffic, my child's sickness or anything else making me late. It was *me*—my failure to anticipate those common and regular events. I was the culprit, and it wasn't cute.

I love being on time now. I am on time to the hairdresser and to pick up my son from school. I am on time to doctor's appointments and lunches with friends. How do I do it? It's so simple. I can't believe I didn't see it sooner. I simply choose to be on time. Choosing to be on time requires that I plan well in advance and take into account obvious issues that could delay me, like snow or children or traffic. I don't have conversations that will hold me up when I can't afford to be delayed. I don't hit the snooze. Ever. I'm not even sure how it works on my current alarm clock. Being on time is no more a character trait than being late was. It's a habit. It's simply a choice I make.

One of the most wonderful things about being on time is how much it honors the people I am meeting. They know that being with them is sufficiently important to me that I would never keep them waiting. Plus, being on time allows me not to hurry, not to speed on the freeway, not to get tense weaving in and out of traffic trying to make up for the extra twenty minutes I spent in bed. And yes, being on time occasionally means being early. I don't mind that a bit. I carry a book with me everywhere I go just for this eventuality. I love having a few minutes to sit in the car to read before a meeting (or to check my e-mail or facebook page).

You Already Know How

Does any of this sound familiar to you? Is being late a habit you've picked up over the years? Maybe your habit is biting your fingernails or checking your phone while someone is talking to you or telling jokes that demean other people: "C'mon. I was just kidding."

Or maybe your habit is getting aggravated with other people's choices when you can't do anything about them. You see a large man at the buffet restaurant eating plate after plate of food, and you can't help judging him. "What does he think he's doing? Can you believe that?!"

Or you hear your spouse blaming his failure to advance at work on his boss when you know it's really his fault, so you judge him, too. "Honey, you know this isn't about your boss. It's about you not going the extra mile. When are you going to accept that?"

These thought patterns are habits too, aren't they, just like being late? And, being habits, they are based on choices—choices you can change.

I know there is a difference between a habit and an addiction. I've heard it explained that a habit is something you have control over, where your will can be exercised to affect change, whereas an addiction involves something more than simple will. I don't pretend to be an expert in this area. I am not a doctor or a scientist or any other person qualified to speak on the subject of behavioral psychology or addiction.

I know of hundreds of books that share documented studies about how people change their lives in the area of addiction and bad habits. They often map out in detail the different steps, the different states of mind involved, etc. Many might be beneficial to you, but as a group, they haven't been to me. I don't want to discourage you from anything that might help, including seeing a doctor or counselor to develop your understanding further, but for me, learning how to stop being late didn't help me to actually do it. Studying how to stop overeating didn't make me stop putting food in my mouth. Researching all about how to exercise did not help me get out there and move! I have discovered that I don't need to be taught how to change a habit. I already know. It's one of those things that you either do or you don't do, but you already know how.

Knowing how doesn't mean it will be easy. Changing a habit requires commitment, motivation—a desire to change. But there is nothing complicated about it. It's as simple as making a choice. You've done it many times before. Think of all the bad habits you've broken in your life. Celebrate them. Get up and do the "I broke a bad habit" dance like I do the "Ethan took his medicine" dance at home when my four-year-old finally takes his medicine. Today, I celebrate breaking the lifelong habit of being late. I did it! I did it! I just made up my mind to do it, and that was it. I went cold turkey on lateness. The same kind of choice could be applied to any habit you want to change—if you have sufficient motivation. Which, let's just be honest, you may not have.

I am not saying that you need to change anything. But if, as you're reading these words, you're thinking of something in particular you want to change in your own life, then that tells me that you have a little mental mosquito about some behavior, some situation, some thought—some choice to make. And if you're thinking about it, perhaps even obsessing over it, that's likely happening for a reason. It's there all the time at the periphery of your mind because you're ready to change it.

Let's bring it on down front and center. "Come on in and sit down for a while, Mr. Habit." Let's allow that thought to have all your mental attention, instead of just the annoying sideline position it's occupied. "Come on in. Step right up, bad habit of yelling at my children whenever I get tired. I'm going to look at you right now." And once it's there, in the front of your mind, you can ask if you have sufficient motivation to change it. Do you? Do you want to stop yelling at them, or is it really not that bad? Do you want to stop eating candy every day, or is it really not that bad? (And it may not be—I'm just asking.) Do you want to stop blaming your ex-husband or your boss or your mother for the way you feel and realize this feeling is *your* feeling? You may not have the motivation. You may like blaming them because then you don't have to take the next step—changing it.

Steps to changing a bad habit (I'm kidding–you don't need these!):

1. What is bugging you?
2. Do you really want to change it—really?
3. STOP DOING IT!!

Forgive me for repeating something you already know, but for those of you who really think it's somebody else's job to make you be on time or clean or happy, let me be very clear: you will change your habits, bad or otherwise, the day you want to change more than you want to continue. In other words, the day you choose to change. I am not aware of a magic formula.

Here is the truth—there is no such thing as a habit you don't want.

The "I don't want to be a slob," or, "I don't want to treat you this way," or "I don't want to overeat," is a lie. You do want to—until you don't. If you ever don't want to, you'll stop. That's how you'll know you don't want to anymore.[2]

> **There is no such thing as a habit you don't want.**

Here's the Good News

So many of the changes we have to handle in life are changes we didn't choose. We didn't choose to get cancer or lose a spouse or lose a job. We didn't have any choice in those life-altering changes. But changing a habit? This is something you totally get to choose. It's all up to you, baby! Finally *you* get to control something. Your life experience, the way you feel, the way you eat and work and live is filled with habits— and they're all completely under your control. The only hard

---

2. These are not my original ideas. I was given the opportunity to listen to the recorded seminars from author Byron Katie who spoke about "Loving What Is."

part is making up your mind. After that, the rest takes care of itself.

Enjoy the new ride you've chosen for yourself. The ride that is always on time, the ride that breathes instead of yells at her kids, the one that reads instead of eats. This is the ride you've seen at the amusement park but didn't think to get on. Perhaps you weren't sure if you were tall enough. But now, now that you've made up your mind and strapped yourself in, the ride is pulling away. Nothing to do now but hang on and see how you like the view from here.

And if you find you don't like it, you know what to do— change it!

CHAPTER TEN
Everything Is Going to Be Okay

I have six simple words I want to share with you: Everything is going to be okay.

It feels so good to hear those words, doesn't it? No matter your age or circumstance, your gender or ethnicity, your challenges or blessings, it feels good on a soul level to hear those words: Everything is going to be okay.

And do you want to know why it feels good? Because they're true! Many of you already know they are. Some of you may just hope they are. Some of you only wish they were, and are doubtful. You think they sound too Pollyannaish to be true. They sound too easy, too trite. Nothing could be that simple.

Except the truth. The truth is always simple, isn't it?

Love your neighbor. Simple.

Do the right thing. Simple.

Forgive. Simple and direct.

When concepts start to get complicated, that's my first clue that we may be veering from the truth. I understand that business transactions sometimes need to be complicated. Stock transfers and technical details may need to be complex, but the truth doesn't. The truth, at the heart of all human interaction, is straightforward. The language is simple.

Everything is going to be okay. And do you know how I know that's true?

Because of change.

If you are in the throes of the worst time in your life, change will heal you. If you feel stuck and cramped and resentful of your responsibilities, hold on. They will change. If you feel overwhelmed by the day-to-day tasks of caring for young children, hang in there. They are growing up and, before you know it, everything will be different. If you feel sick of being broke all the time and wish you had money to be able to do something for a change, patience, patience. Someday, you will. Play your cards even a little bit right, and you will. Because in the end, change will set you free.

This, Too, Shall Pass

I remember the nights after my first son was born, those long, terrifying nights when I felt completely alone and unable to be the person I needed to be, the mother I needed to be. I'm sure, looking back now, that much of that feeling was hormonal, but at the time, it felt like the end of the world. I simply couldn't care for this child. He wouldn't nurse—which had to be my fault. He wouldn't sleep, my fault. He wouldn't do anything except cry, whether he was lying down or swinging in the swing or being held.

And in his endless screams, I began to think that I would never smile again, not really. I assumed every other mother had this stuff down, this mother thing. Every other mom just whipped that baby up, nursed him, changed him, reswaddled him and back down he went, out like a light. I was jealous of all these other imaginary moms and what I assumed was their easy competence. My jealousy felt like anger when 3:00 or 4:00 A.M. would come around and I hadn't been to sleep yet and all the good reruns were over.

Then my mother reminded me, "This, too, shall pass." I think my husband had tried to remind me of that too, but I wasn't hearing anything he had to say that week.

"This, too, shall pass." No matter what the pain, no matter how intense, how dark the night, this, too, shall pass. If you are reading these words with a heart so heavy the tears are coming even now, let me hold your hand as my mother held mine.

"This, too, shall pass." If you feel rejected, ignored, invisible to the people you love the most, and you think you just can't live another day without being seen by somebody, anybody, this, too, shall pass. Even pain, every kind of pain, will eventually pass. And I'm not just saying this to make you feel better. I know that if you're in real pain, you are well past platitudes from some author you don't even know. You don't have to take my word for it. I have proof.

Change. Change is why this too shall pass. Change, that constant, unavoidable, and completely natural process will, in the end, remove our pain. It will ease our minds, show us the way, introduce us to people we need to meet, help us out of ditches we've dug so deep we can't see the top anymore. That's the power of change. And it comes whether you think to invite it or not. It comes no matter what your state of mind. It comes because that is the divine way of things. You cannot keep the experience of life the same, even when you want to. Change comes. It may already be coming, but you've got too many tears in your eyes to see it just yet. Go wash your face. You'll see better in the morning.

Doesn't the experience of your own life tell you this is true? Do you remember the worst pain you've ever felt, and I'm talking physical pain now? When was that? Was it in childbirth or when you broke a limb or had a surgery? Can you re-create that pain in your mind? Probably not exactly. No matter how intense it was at the time, so much has passed since then that you just can't conjure it up. Do the best you can. Remember that pain? I bet you feel utterly different right now. You're probably not crying out for God to save you right at this moment like you were when labor kicked in. Now remember the worst emotional pain you've ever felt. You don't have to hang out there for long. Just remember it long enough to feel how different your heart feels right now. I bet when that was happening, when she first left you and you thought you didn't want to live, you did not see any way your life could come to the place it is now. And yet, here you are. How did that happen?

Change.

Change is the gift that keeps on giving. It is the second chance, the do-over, the eternal mulligan.

Years ago, when I was an attorney, there were clients in our office who had been convicted of business crimes and were facing the terrifying experience of loss of job, loss of personal fortune, loss of reputation and goodwill in their communities. As they opened the morning paper, they'd see articles about their crimes. They'd call the law office, frantic. Could we get the papers to stop printing these stories? No, we couldn't. But this, too, shall pass, we told them. They couldn't feel it at the time, but we would tell them that people have terribly short memories, and that, before they knew it, this painful phase in their lives would be over, and they would have a chance to take what they'd learned and use it for good, or let it fester.

Which would it be? The one thing for sure is that it would not remain the same. They would not be the headline forever. They would be old news because the news, like everything else, is constantly changing.

EGBOK

Six little words: Everything is going to be okay.

They have such magic in them, don't they? It's what wives ask their husbands to say when they're worried about the health of a child or the state of the world, what employees want to hear from their managers after coworkers have been laid off and departments have been closed. It's what nations want to hear from presidents after a horrible storm or an attack. There is power in that simple phrase.

Two popular radio announcers in Los Angeles in the '80s used to say "EGBOK" all the time. "Hey—give me an EG-BOK," one would say to the other.

"EGBOK," the other would respond with enthusiasm.

EGBOK—everything is going to be okay.

It won't be the same, that's for sure. But it's going to be okay.

CHAPTER ELEVEN

"Be the Change You Want to See in the World"

MAHATMA GANDHI

What will you do now? Now that you may look differently at both the personal change happening to just you and the communal change happening to all of us in the world? What will you do with the energy you used to devote to the fear of change?

Will you build something? Will you help someone? Will you live differently? Will you interpret differently the news of change in the world? Perhaps a development in India, China, or elsewhere will feel welcome instead of threatening.

Look at how we as a planet are growing and learning. When you see the change from dependency on fossil fuels to development of reusable energy, you may see it differently than you used to and want to embrace the change. When you learn of other cultures, other people who wear different clothing, who eat different foods and celebrate different milestones, you might think how they, too, are subjected every day to the constant that is universal—change. Imagine how rocking the change must be in a country like China, where the way of life millions have been comfortable with for centuries is replaced by technology overnight. And we thought *our* lives were full of change!

It is my hope that we might all live the wisdom of Mahatma Gandhi when he encouraged, "Be the change you wish to see in the world."

Change is a powerful wind to be harnessed by you.

What change do you wish for? How can you live it? The concept seems so simple. If you wish for peace in the world, live peacefully with your children and coworkers and neighbors. Wish them well. Forgive them easily. Give them a hand up when they need it without keeping score.

If you wish for beauty in the world, plant flowers around your home, wear beautiful clothing, contribute to community gardens and aviaries. If you wish for the end of suffering, nurse the sick in your home and in your neighborhood, even if you may catch what they've got. Nurse them with your words and pies and loving arms.

What do you wish for? Change is a powerful wind to be

harnessed by you. How will you use it? In which direction will you guide it? What light will you turn on with its power?

It Takes Just One

When I look at some of the greatest changes in human history, I realize that they have often been brought on by one individual. One person named Jesus Christ gave up his life for all of us. One person named George Washington led a ragtag army against the might of the English empire in order to establish a free America. One person named Abraham Lincoln acted upon the belief that a nation divided cannot stand. One woman named Rosa Parks made up her mind not to give up her bus seat to a white man. The courage and faith of these individuals changed everything. Oh, what power in just one person!

How will you use your power? Toward what worthy goal will you apply your strength and energy? You don't have to be loud or smart or rich or famous to be the change you want to see in the world. You don't have to be elected or educated or eloquent to change the world. You just have to take an action step.

People who follow Gandhi's call to action see change as a verb. Change is not just a slogan they see on campaign posters or coins they get back at the convenience store. Change is something they do, all the time, every day. They effect change. They invite change. They embrace change. The word Gandhi used was "be"—be the change you want to see in the world. He didn't say "think about" the change, or "acknowledge" the change, or "study" the change—he said *be* the change.

And being something that you're currently not requires action.

Change Is Messy

The action change requires cannot wait until the conditions are perfect to begin. This is one of the mistakes we so easily make. We put off embracing change until everything is just right.

"As soon as I have a little bit saved up, *then* I'll donate to that cause that means so much to me." Donate now. You'll never have enough saved up.

"As soon as the kids are grown, *then* I'll get involved with the homeless shelter. I've always wanted to work with homeless people." Don't wait. The kids will be fine. In fact, they'll be better off now with a parent who sets such a personal and powerful example of loving one's neighbor.

"I wish I had a better relationship with my sister, but she lives so far away." That's why there's e-mail and facebook and Twitter and . . . need I go on?

Yes, change is messy. All good things are. But, hey, messes

can be cleaned up. I've never met a mess I didn't know how to clean (or couldn't call somebody who did know how). Get in there and get your hands dirty. Why not? You don't want to keep your house and your hands so clean that you miss all the fun, do you? And you don't want to keep your life so pristine that you miss all the change. Don't turn your life into a museum. Let it be a playground of thought and ideas and action.

We Cannot Change Others, Only Ourselves

The only change I discourage you from acting upon is the desire to change others. It won't work. I've tried it—lots of times. Never worked. We simply cannot change others.

We're not meant to. That's why we fail so miserably every time we try. We can't make our spouses different or our children more appreciative or our bosses more patient. We can't make our friends less irritating or our neighbors quieter or our waiters less uppity.

Be the change you want to see in others.

It just won't work. Apply no energy, dear reader, to trying to change anyone. Take any energy you've mistakenly applied to that endeavor and immediately apply it where it belongs.

Change yourself.

If you wish your husband were more thoughtful, be more thoughtful. If you wish your daughter were more grateful,

127

be more grateful. If you wish your coworkers were more efficient, be more efficient. See how this works? Be the change you want to see in others. Be the change you wish to see in the world.

It will feel completely natural when you embrace this concept. You will be aligning yourself with a law of nature. You are the embodiment of change. Your reflection is a vision of change, change and light.

You are change, breathing.

ACKNOWLEDGMENTS

The best ideas in this book are not mine, or at least not mine alone. My husband, Aaron, is the source of most good things in my life, including my understanding of change. He is my first and best editor and contributor. I am also grateful to the contributions of my brother David Dickson III, who helped me formulate my ideas at the beginning stages of this book. My father David Dickson Jr., my sister Connie Hite, her daughter (my namesake) Amanda Hite, my son Cameron Wilhelm, my friends Cinda Morgan, Carol Ferguson, and Shela Barker, and my radio partner Grant Nielsen also contributed many good thoughts that have found their way to these pages.

These words would never have made their way to print

were it not for the faith Sheri Dew placed in me. Her friendship and support humbles me. I love you, Sheri.

I am also so grateful for the support and counsel that my project manager, Jana Erickson, gave me. She shaped this work into something so much better than I thought it could be. Jana and my editor, Lisa Mangum, were integral to the preparation of this work. I thank them. I would also like to thank Gail Halladay for her enthusiasm and support, Rachael Ward for her typesetting work, Richard Erickson for his art direction, and Sheryl Dickert Smith for her wonderful design; the cover makes me smile every time I see it.

I am so grateful to my coworkers at KSL Radio who were patient and encouraging at every step along the way. Thank you to my Vice President and General Manager Chris Redgrave, Program Director Kevin LaRue, and coworkers Maria Shilaos, Scott Seeger, Dave Mecham, Doug Wright, Sue Kelley, Zak Kindrachuk, and Von Coffman.

This book is the compilation of ideas developed over a lifetime, most of which were taught me by my accidental professors—my children—Laurel, Ashley, Cameron, Ethan, and Aiden. It would likely never have been written had it not been for a deep desire to help my daughter—Ashley Wilhelm—achieve her dreams. And so it is to Ashley that I dedicate these pages with the hope that it aids her in her journey.

SOURCES

Bernstein, Leonard. In *This I Believe.* Edited by Jay Allison and Dan Gediman. New York: Henry Holt, 2007.

Buck, Pearl S. http://en.thinkexist.com/quotes/Pearl_S._Buck/

Carnegie, Dale. http://en.thinkexist.com/search/searchquotation .asp?search=opinion+still&q=author%3A%22Dale +Carnegie%22

Darwin, Charles. http://en.thinkexist.com/quotes/charles_darwin/

de Bono, Edward. http://www.brainyquote.com/quotes/authors/e/ edward_de_bono.html

Gandhi, Mahatma. http://thinkexist.com/quotes/mahatma _gandhi/

Jefferson, Thomas. http://en.thinkexist.com/search/search quotation.asp?search=barbarous+ancestors&q=author%3A%22 Thomas+Jefferson%22

Sources

Lincoln, Abraham. http://en.thinkexist.com/search/search
quotation.asp?search=act+anew&q=author%3A%22Abraham
+Lincoln%22

Peale, Norman Vincent. http://en.thinkexist.com/quotes/Norman
_Vincent_Peale/

Picasso, Pablo. http://en.thinkexist.com/search/searchquotation
.asp?search=learn&q=author%3A%22Pablo+Picasso%22

Scrooge. DVD. Directed by Ronald Neame. Hollywood, CA:
Paramount, 1970.

Thoreau, Henry David. http://thinkexist.com/quotes/henry_david
_thoreau/3.html

Wilson, Harold. http://en.thinkexist.com/quotes/Harold _Wilson/

Wilson, Woodrow. http://en.thinkexist.com/quotes/woodrow
_t._wilson/3.html